The Potter's Craft

The Potter's Craft

BY

CHARLES F. BINNS

*Late Director of New York State School of Clay-Working
and Ceramics from 1900 to 1932; former superintendent
in the Royal Porcelain Works, Worcester, England.*

THIRD EDITION—THIRD PRINTING

D. VAN NOSTRAND COMPANY, Inc.

TORONTO   NEW YORK   LONDON

NEW YORK

D. Van Nostrand Company, Inc., 250 Fourth Avenue, New York 3

TORONTO

D. Van Nostrand Company (Canada), Ltd., 228 Bloor Street, Toronto

LONDON

Macmillan & Company, Ltd., St. Martin's Street, London, W.C. 2

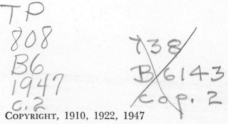

First Published May 1947

Reprinted November 1947, December 1948

PRINTED IN THE UNITED STATES OF AMERICA
BY LANCASTER PRESS, INC., LANCASTER, PA.

A BOOK is written, not to multiply the voice merely, not to carry it merely, but to perpetuate it. The author has something to say which he perceives to be true and useful, or helpfully beautiful. So far as he knows, no one has yet said it; so far as he knows, no one else can say it. He is bound to say it clearly and melodiously if he may; clearly, at all events.

—*Ruskin.*

PREFACE TO THE THIRD EDITION

MANY students and craftsmen in this and other countries who practice the craft of the potter will bear witness to the fact that this book has fulfilled the purpose set forth by the author in his preface to the first edition. The "sign-posts and occasional warnings" of thirty years ago are still timely and of value, and testify to the farsightedness and vitality of the book—the words of one potter to another.

New materials and new methods are now available, making necessary some changes in this third edition. The revisors, ceramists in their own right, have conscientiously preserved the original intention and quality of the author's words.

To those who believe as the author did that "the path to strength and beauty leads through fire" this new edition of *The Potter's Craft* will be welcome.

ELSIE BINNS

Alfred, New York
February, 1947

PREFACE TO THE FIRST EDITION

THIS Book is the outcome of an experience extending over a period of thirty-six years. Twenty years ago it would have been impossible, for the science of ceramics was not then born. Ten years ago it would have been wasted for the Artist-potter in America had not arrived, but now the individual workers are many and the science is well established.

Written teaching must be imperfect, but I have endeavored to set down the exact methods by which my students are taught, in the hope that those who cannot secure personal instruction may read and understand.

As far as possible didactic statements have been avoided and the attempt has been made to lead every student to experiment and to think for himself. In other words, I have tried to erect sign-posts and occasional warnings rather than to remove all obstacles from the road.

C. F. B.

Alfred, N. Y.
January, 1910.

CONTENTS

INTRODUCTION

MANY times it has been proved, in the history of the world, that it is not possible to force a reform or a novelty upon an unwilling people. Such things are organic. In order to live, they must grow; and in order to grow, they must live. No attempt will be made, therefore, in these pages to foster an idea or propound a thought which may exist only in the predilection of the author.

It is not intended, in these lines, to consider what are generally termed the Fine Arts, painting and sculpture. These are perfectly competent to take care of themselves and, indeed, the author can make no claim to an ability to discuss them.

In the field of applied design, however, there are certain principles to be observed—principles, moreover, which are frequently lost sight of because of the lamentable separation of the functions of the artist and artificer.

It should not be a purpose of any craft to make pieces merely as an exhibition of skill. This is done sometimes by clever workmen, but it may be laid down as a law that a production of the nature of a tour de force, an object which simply excites wonder at the skill of the worker, is undignified and meretricious. It is akin to the work of certain painters who delight in painting marble or velvet so as to exhibit a perfect texture only, and is but one degree removed from the skill of the pavement artist who, with colored chalk, draws a lamb chop or a banana in such a manner that the real article seems to be lying on the ground at his feet.

It cannot be too strongly emphasized that to imitate one material in another is false from every point of view. Clay is sufficient in itself. There are so many effects possible in ceramics which are not possible in any other medium that it is entirely superfluous to seek imitative effects.

Novelty in itself is no claim to consideration; in fact on being shown some product of which it is said, "Nothing like it has ever been seen before," the temptation is great to respond, "May its like never be seen again."

Novelty apart, there must be a sense of form, a term which includes outline, proportion, structure. There must be fitness to purpose. A chair must invite the sitter, a carpet must lie flat, a vase must stand securely and must hold water—a vase which will not hold water is technically imperfect and the bête noire of the conscientious potter. There must be fitness to material. A porcelain vase is required to be light, graceful and refined. A piece of ruder pottery may be no less satisfactory if it exhibits vigor, strength and solidity.

Another point of fitness is concerned in the correspondence between size and weight. It often happens that one takes hold of a piece of pottery and experiences a shock. The mind unconsciously forms an estimate of what the weight will be but the piece does not respond. The effort put forth in accordance with the appearance of the object either lifts it suddenly into the air or fails to raise it from the table.

The artist critic takes note of these things; he must have courage to destroy that which is below standard, and self-denial to resist the temptation to sell an unworthy product, and he must possess enthusiasm, skill, discrimination and infinite patience.

The country needs craftsmen of this type and for them there is an important work. It is for them that these words are written, and in the hope that some may be stimulated, guided, helped and encouraged the counsel of a fellow craftsman is offered.

Chapter I

POTTERY

IT must always be an open question how much credit for artistic feeling can be given to primitive races. The production of pottery was, at first, the supplying of a need. Clay offered a medium for the making of household utensils which were at once fireproof and impervious. The work does not belong strictly to the earliest stages of civilization but is a development of advancing refinement.

Crude and unprepared clays were used for the most part but the makers could scarcely have been conscious of the charming color-play produced by the burning of a red clay in a smoky fire. The pottery of the Indians is artistic in the sense of being an expression of an indigenous art and much of it is beautiful, but whether the makers possessed any real appreciation of beauty is open to doubt.

The pottery was exclusively the work of the women. No wheel was employed but the ware was mainly constructed by coiling. The base, not usually flat, was made by pressing a small bat of clay into a rounded depression —a hollow in a stone, for example—or a small basket. This may well have been the first step toward working with molds. Long strips of clay were rolled under the hands and made of uniform size and these were then coiled in spiral form, the rolls being welded together with water. After proceeding a certain height the walls of the growing jar would become weak under their own

1

weight. The piece would then be set aside to undergo a partial hardening upon which the work would be carried forward another stage. The shape being completed and partially dried, the maker would work over the whole surface with stones or simple tools until the marks of the coils had disappeared and the walls had reached a sufficient thinness. A great deal of skill was exercised in accomplishing this.

Many of the Indian forms are transitional. The basket, the gourd and the bark-made jar suggested their shapes to the potter; indeed it is sometimes evident that clay vessels were constructed as linings to wicker forms, the outer layer of twigs being burned off afterward. The firing was performed in the open flame without any protection, a fact which accounts for the great irregularity found in quality and color.

The decorations used by the Indian women were of the type common to unglazed wares. The clay was incised or embossed and natural earths were used as pigments. This accounts in great measure for the fitness which may be observed in aboriginal decoration. There is an absence of artificial coloring, nor is there any straining after effect, but instead there is shown a sober strength and a sane expression of values which would do credit to a modern designer.

America is fortunate in possessing abundant relics of primitive times but it cannot be doubted that in other lands similar work was done, making allowance, of course, for the characteristic variations in national traits. The potter's craft is of such a nature, using an omnipresent material and requiring the minimum of tools, that almost every nation on the globe has practiced it. In some it has never been developed beyond the narrow limits of the stone age, in others it has reached the utmost perfection of cultured skill.

For perfection of quality in crude pottery, no ware has ever surpassed that of Greece. It is not practicable here to deal with the numerous branches and sub-branches of Greek pottery; let it suffice for the present purpose to speak of only two main groups. In the first, the background of the decoration was supplied by the tint of the bare clay; in the second, this tint afforded the color of the decoration itself, the background being covered with a black pigment. To speak briefly these groups are known as black-figured and red-figured wares.

The wheel was early adopted by the Grecian potters as a means of producing form and, although molds were sometimes used, the wheel was, to all intents and purposes, the sole method of manufacture. Greek pottery is once fired. Birch classes it as glazed terra cotta, but the glaze is nothing more than the black pigment with which the decoration is carried out. The uncolored part of the clay is not glazed but polished with a hard tool. Probably some famous potters employed assistants either to make the pieces or to decorate but it does not appear that there was any reproduction, at least during the best period. At first primitive ideas prevailed. Geometric designs were succeeded by rhythmic friezes of beasts and birds done in black. When the human figure made its appearance the faces were all in profile with full-fronting eye while the prominent details of feature and drapery were scratched with a sharp point before burning.

The change of method to red on black gave much

wider scope for the treatment of the human figure, rendered a fuller expression possible and enlarged the power of pictorial action. Great skill in drawing was manifested and details of both drapery and features were expressed with great care by means of the brush.

Such was the state of the art when the decadence set in and the work fell into the hands of plagiarists and charlatans. Meretricious coloring and gaudy ornament succeeded the refinement and restraint of the earlier days and so the art perished.

To the inventive power of the Romans the ceramic art owes more than one novelty. It would appear that the desideratum of the early days was a black ware. Homer in his hymn wrote:

> "Pay me my price, potters, and I will sing.
> Attend, O Pallas, and with lifted arm protect their ovens,
> Let all their cups and sacred vessels blacken well
> And baked with good success yield them
> Both fair renown and profit."

The Greeks accomplished this blackening by means of a pigment, the Romans secured a similar result by a manipulation of the fire.

It is well known that the oxide of iron which imparts to the clay a red color will, if burned in what is known as a "reducing" fire, turn black. This is accomplished by keeping the air supply at the lowest possible point and the effect is heightened by the smoke which is partly absorbed by the clay. This black ware is known as Upchurch pottery from the name of a locality in England where large quantities have been found, but numerous examples occur in Germany and, indeed, wherever the Roman hosts encamped.

A second type of pottery is called Castor ware and consists of a dark clay upon which the decoration is traced in clay of a lighter color. The decoration was applied as a slip or cream and hence was the forerunner of the modern slip painting or *pâte-sur-pâte*. This ware is well worth a study. The decorations consisted largely of conventional borders and panels but it is specially notable on account of the free use of motives drawn from daily life. One of the commonest scenes depicted is the hunt of hare or stag, the animals and trees being often woven into an almost conventional frieze.

The most valued type of Roman pottery seems to have been the Aretine or Samian ware. This is a bright red color and possesses an extremely thin glaze. A particular clay was evidently used, but all knowledge of its source has been lost.

With the importation of Chinese porcelain by the Dutch the whole trend of pottery manufacture was changed. No longer was black a desirable color, white was seen to be much more delicate and beautiful and henceforth the endeavor of the potter was to produce a ware which should be as nearly like porcelain as possible. The crudeness of the clay kept this ideal from being realized, but various expedients were adopted and gradually better results were obtained.

Throughout the East a type of white pottery was made which, although stimulated by the Chinese example, may have been a relic of the knowledge of the Egyptians. A crude clay was coated with a white preparation, possibly ground quartz, and upon this there were painted conventional designs in sombre colors. A clear glaze covered the whole and imparted to the colors a beautiful quality as of pebbles under water. The nature of the glaze is made evident by the hues assumed by the metallic oxides employed as colorants. Copper oxide affords a turquoise blue, manganese, a wine purple, and iron, a brick red. If the glaze had contained any considerable amount of lead oxide, these colors would have been quite different; copper would have produced green, manganese, dark brown, and iron, yellowish brown. The iron pigment was evidently a clay, sometimes spoken of as Armenian bole. The red color is always in raised masses because if a thin wash had been used the color would have yielded to the action of the glaze.

This ware, commonly called Oriental *engobe* ware, affords a fruitful study. Effects similar in character were produced by the late Theodore Deck of Paris, but no considerable use of the ancient methods has ever been attempted.

The use of tin and lead in glazing was known to the Arabian and Moorish potters but these ingredients were not abundant in the East. When, however, the Moorish hosts conquered a part of Spain in the twelfth century it was found that both lead and tin were available. The result was the development of the enameled ware known by the generic name Maiolica. Some have maintained that this was first made in Italy but the name is derived from the island of Maiorca from which much of the pottery was exported. The famous Alhambra vase remains as a monument to the skill of the Hispano-Moresque craftsmen, but it was the Italian artists of the Renaissance who brought the enameled wares to perfection. The interest here is artistic and technical rather than historical, but no one can study the work of the period without learning something of Luca della Robbia and Giorgio Andreoli, of Gubbio and Pesaro and Castel Durante.

The use of lead in the glaze proved seductive. It simplified the technical problems and provided a brilliant surface but alas! the colors suffered and one by one they succumbed. The blue of cobalt, however, proved indestructible and so, when the technical knowledge of the South met the traditions borrowed from the Chinese, there was born, in the little town of Delft in Holland, the blue enameled ware which has since been known by the name of its native place.

As to the technical details of the production of Delft ware a great deal of information is available. The clay used contained a goodly proportion of lime, and this served to hold the enamel in perfect union with the body. The decoration was painted in cobalt blue upon the unburned surface of the enamel. This was, in a measure, courting a difficulty but it is the glory of the craft that a difficulty is cheerfully accepted if in the overcoming there is found success. If the Delft potters had burned their enamel in order to make the painting easy, the world would never have enjoyed the tender tone of blue for which this pottery is famous. By painting the blue color over the powdery enamel, a more perfect union of enamel and color was accomplished than would have been possible by any other means. This fact alone is sufficient to account for the unsatisfactory nature of the modern, so-called, Delft. Difficulties have been avoided rather than met and the success of the early masters has eluded their recent followers.

Much of the pottery made in France in the seventeenth century was inspired by the Italian Renaissance. In fact the word faience is due to the avowed intention of the manufacturers of Nevers to copy the enameled pottery of Faenza. Almost the only novelty of the time was the inversion, by the Nevers potters, of the Delft idea. Instead of a white enamel with a blue decoration, they used, in part, a blue ground with a decoration in white. It is not known that this variation found acceptance in any other place but in many localities, notably at Rouen, the manufacture of enameled wares was pursued with great success. The only real difference between the wares of Spain, Italy and France, lies in the decorative treatment. Sometimes the emphasis was laid upon lusters, sometimes on blue and white and again upon polychrome painting. In one place there was an extensive use made of pictorial treatment, in another all was conventional. The differences are interesting to a student or a collector but to the craftsman enameled pottery affords but one, although by no means an unimportant, means of expression.

France, however, gave birth to two interesting departures from the beaten track; the so-called Henri deux ware, and the faience of Bernard Palissy. Important as these are to the ceramist, it is a remarkable fact that neither of them had any appreciable influence upon the art as a whole nor did they leave any descendants.

A good deal of controversy has raged around the pottery commonly known as Henri II, some authorities claiming that it should be called Faience d'Oiron, and others assigning to it the name Saint Porchaire. It was, quite evidently, the production of an individual or group of individuals who had no connection with ordinary pottery manufacture, and the small quantity produced is evidence that it was made for personal pleasure. The name

Henri II is undoubtedly satisfactory, for it was made in the reign of the second Henry and some pieces bear the monogram of the king. On the other hand H may be the initial of Helene d'Hengest, who occupied the chateau d'Oiron and who had in her employ one Bernard who filled the position of librarian. The style of the work seems to indicate a devotion to books, for the patterns are suggestive of book-binding tool work but were not produced in the same way. The ware was made of a natural cream-colored clay and the shapes were modeled with great skill. Upon the plain surface patterns were tooled or incised and the hollows thus formed were filled in with dark-colored clays. The whole was then covered with a clear lead glaze which afforded a finish very much like modern earthenware.

The origin of this work is a matter of little more than academic interest but the technical details are of such importance as to be well worth a study. The ware is original and unique. No pottery, either before or since, has approached it in method, and the quality of most of the pieces is all that could be desired. Such was the elaboration of detail that no price could have been set upon the ware and it was evidently not made for sale. A distinct growth in style can be traced. The first pieces were somewhat archaic and even crude but as skill was acquired greater perfection was attained. As is too often the case, however, the skillful hand overreached itself and the later pieces are loaded with meretricious detail in many colors. There are only about fifty pieces known and these are equally divided between the museums of France and England.

Bernard Palissy was a versatile genius but is here only

considered as a potter. He states in his records that he was inspired by seeing an enameled cup. It was at one time supposed that this cup was of Italian maiolica but later authorities incline to the belief that it was a piece of Chinese porcelain which Palissy supposed to have been enameled. No white clay was known to him but enameled wares were quite accessible. It can scarcely be believed that maiolica was a novelty but it can easily be understood that a piece of white porcelain, viewed in the light of the contemporary knowledge of enamels, would appear of marvellous quality.

Palissy essayed to imitate this wonder but attacked the problem from the standpoint of an opaque glaze. He spent fifteen years in experimenting but never realized his ideal. He did, however, produce a palette of marvelous colored enamels. He was a close student of nature and modeled all kinds of natural objects, glazing them in the proper hues. He also designed and made vases and service pieces, some with figure embossments. The story of his struggles is readily accessible to those who are interested.

Palissy left little or no impression upon the ceramic art of his time but in recent years some work has been done in colored glazes fusible at a low temperature. This ware is sometimes sold under the name of maiolica but it is more nearly an imitation of Palissy. The main difference between the two types is that, while the maiolica or tin-glazed pottery of Spain, Italy and France consisted for the most part of a white enameled surface upon which painting was applied, Palissy used little or no white enamel but decorated his wares with tinted glazes which themselves supplied the colors.

In the low countries and the German states there was made the striking and original pottery known as *Grès de Flandres*. The clay was of the type commonly used for the manufacture of stoneware and appears in three colors, brown, gray and cream. The ware was made on the wheel and embossments more or less elaborate were subsequently added. The unique feature consisted in the method of applying the glaze. This was simply common salt, thrown into the heated kiln and volatilized. The salt vapor bathed the glowing pottery and combined with its substance, thus producing the delightful orange-skin texture known as salt glaze.

The knowledge of this method was conveyed to England in the seventeenth century and gained wide acceptance there. The English potters preferred to use clays which were almost white, and after glazing, a decoration in brilliant colors was sometimes added. Naturalistic treatment was not attempted but conventionalized subjects were used with almost the effect of jewelry. The temperature at which this work can be produced varies with the clay. Many fusible clays will take a salt glaze but the beauty of the product depends to a large extent upon the purity of the body. This necessitates a hard fire, for white-burning clays always need a high temperature for vitrification. The early potteries of England were dependent largely upon clay effects. Some little enameled ware was made and is known as English Delft; but the bulk of the work was slip painted, incised, marbled or embossed. Each of these methods is capable of an intelligent application and all are within the reach of the artist-potter.

CHAPTER II

PORCELAIN

THE production of porcelain is the goal of the potter. The pure white of the clay and the possibility of unlimited fire treatment exert a profound influence upon the imagination while the difficulties of manipulation only serve to stimulate the energy of the enthusiast. For present purposes not much is to be learned from the soft porcelains of France nor from the bone china of England. German and French hard porcelain are but developments of the Chinese idea and therefore need not be studied apart from their prototype.

The earliest date of Chinese porcelain is unknown. The records of the nation are very ancient but their meaning is often obscured by the fact that in the Chinese language the same word was used of old to denote both porcelain and earthenware. There seems to be a general agreement, however, that the evolution of Chinese pottery from soft earthenware to stoneware and then to porcelain was a gradual development extending over several centuries. In technical perfection and skill of execution the art reached its height during the fourteenth and fifteenth centuries. The Sung wares of the tenth to twelfth centuries are noted for their simple forms, spontaneous style and subtle colors and textures. These earlier porcelains offer a wealth of inspiration for the serious modern potter.

Broadly it may be stated that two methods prevailed. In the former the glaze itself was charged with color or the coloring matter was applied to the clay beneath the glaze. In the latter the porcelain was finished as to body and glaze and the decoration was applied at a subsequent and much lighter burn.

The first named class is called single-colored porcelain; the second has several names such as the famille rose and famille verte as defined by Jacquemart.

In the single-color class it is evident that the potters were not at all sure of their results. In many museums there are to be found examples of ox-blood red, more or less fine, and, with them, other pieces which were intended to be red but which failed in the fire. The wonder is, in these cases, that the pieces, even though failures, are beautiful. The knowledge required for the production of these wares is largely scientific; at the same time it is not to be believed that the Chinese had any special scientific training. They evidently traveled a long and tortuous path before the goal was reached, in fact, they often fell short of it altogether, but they had plenty of time and unlimited patience. The modern potter is, if less patient, more fortunate in that the course has been marked out with more or less accuracy and, if the landmarks of science be heeded, a certain degree of success may be attained.

This single-color work is the true field of the ceramist. Anyone possessing the power of using a pencil, and with a large stock of patience, may produce over-glaze decoration, but to prepare glazes of many hues and to consign them unprotected to the fury of the furnace, requires skill, patience, courage and enthusiasm.

During the last fifty years a new school has arisen which combines in a measure the advantages of the two

Chinese methods. Colors are prepared from refractory materials and upon clay or soft burned biscuit ware, scenes, in more or less conventional form, are painted, or else a design purely conventional in character is applied by the artist. The ware is then glazed and subjected to the severe fire which all porcelain undergoes. The result is that the porcelain and the painting are united in a sense that can never be the case with overglaze treatment. The colors become part of a purely ceramic unit; the spirit of the artist is fixed by the fire.

To this class belong the porcelain of Copenhagen and the recent product of Sevres. These, of course, represent the result of much arduous training and many tedious experiments. Both the training and the experiments are necessary to some extent for every worker, not only because pottery clays vary much in composition, but because individuality can only be obtained by the preparation, in the laboratory, of the desired compounds.

The Chinese, doubtless, stumbled upon many of their successes by accident, helped by the fact that the character of the fire employed influenced many of their colors. This will be explained in a later chapter. They were, however, quick to seize upon that which was good. Many fanciful names were given to the rarest colors, such as "the violet of wild apples," "liquid dawn" and "the red of the bean blossom." This idea has been carried further in France by the invention of such names as *"Sang-de-boeuf," "Sang-de-poulet," "clair-de-lune,"* etc., and pursued in this country in "Peach blow."

In the over-glaze treatment, the type named "famille verte" is characterized by a clear green glaze or enamel over a design in black. The whole is painted over the porcelain glaze and the green enamel is so soft that it is often decomposed on the surface. When a broad black mass is covered with green the decomposition gives rise to prismatic colors and occasions the term "raven's wing black." Some of this ware has also been gilded but the gold lines have disappeared and can only be located by the slight dullness of the enamel where they once were. Well known to collectors also are the rose-back plates. These belong to the "famille rose" in which the characteristic note is a delicate rose pink. This color is prepared from gold and when it is placed upon the back of an egg-shell plate a tender rosy transparency is imparted to the piece. One of the best known of the single colors is the pale sea green named celadon by the French. This color in China was called "the sky after rain" and was considered both rare and valuable.

The porcelain of Copenhagen is the product of scientific skill and artistic taste. In the studios attached to the Royal Manufactory there has grown up a tradition of work and criticism which is fostered by ladies of birth and position. Many of these paint upon the porcelain themselves and so constitute a school which has become world famous.

Natural objects are, for the most part, chosen and, as the palette of colors is quite limited and low in key, owing to the intense fire, a tone of quiet atmosphere pervades the painting. This is accentuated by the use of the air-brush to distribute a ground color upon the ware in graduated strength.

From this brief review it will be seen that the interest in the manufacture of porcelain lies not so much in variety as in the value of individual results. In the pottery described in the previous chapter a great many different clays were used and each one proved suggestive to the potter.　In porcelain, on the other hand, the body clay is almost identical wherever prepared, the requirement of a white translucent paste being paramount.

CHAPTER III

THE NATURE AND PROPERTIES OF CLAY

CLAY differs from earth and soil in that it possesses certain characteristics which these do not possess. Its distribution is very wide but for the most part it lies concealed from view. In certain parts of the country it is so abundant that it breaks through the surface or is exposed as an outcrop but usually it is covered by the soil which supports vegetation. Unless the subsoil consists of sand it is easy to expose a clay by plowing or digging with a spade. It usually appears as a greenish or bluish substance of close and uniform structure. The texture is sometimes smooth but more often numerous small stones are found imbedded in the mass. Such clays as are commonly found can be used for the manufacture of some kind of pottery but in the great majority of cases the ware will be red when fired because the clay contains a proportion of oxide of iron. A pure clay does not contain this and therefore becomes white or nearly white in the kiln.

Pure clay, known as clay base or clay substance, forms a part of all natural clays, although sometimes only a small part. It consists of silica, alumina and water in a state of combination and is thus known as a hydrous aluminium silicate. While this substance is very common as an ingredient of ordinary clay, it is rarely found alone or uncontaminated. Commercial or workable clays may be said to consist of clay base and sand, with or without other impurities such as lime and oxide of iron. For working purposes it may be granted that the potter has to deal with a mixture of clay and sand. But sand is not a definite expression. It may vary both physically and chemically within wide limits. The physical nature has to do with condition, the chemical with composition. Thus a sand may be almost as coarse as gravel or as fine as the clay itself. It may be a pure quartz sand or it may be a crushed rock of almost any composition. The former is known as quartz, the latter as feldspar or feldspathic sand because it approaches in composition the group of minerals known as feldspars. Each of these ingredients, clay, quartz and feldspar, has an important part to play in the transformation of clay into pottery. Few of the clays used in making white pottery possess these ingredients in the correct proportions so that it becomes necessary to make a mixture in which the necessary proportions will be found.

For successful pottery making three properties are demanded in a clay. First, plasticity. Without this, clay could not be shaped at all. It constitutes the obedience of a clay to the forming influence whether hand or mold. The necessity for this quality may be illustrated by the proverb "Making ropes of sand" as an example of the impossible. Sand, possessing no plasticity, cannot be shaped or made to hold together.

The second property is porosity. A clay which exhibits a high degree of plasticity can be easily shaped but it cannot be safely dried. The water of plasticity cannot escape and therefore the clay warps and cracks. The function of porosity is to prevent this. A porous clay permits the water to escape freely and the clay can be dried without damage. This condition is produced by the admixture of sand or by the presence of sand in a natural clay.   A coarse sand is more effective than a fine sand but a sand that is too coarse will interfere with delicate working while a sand that is too fine approximates the action of the clay itself and produces a substance which is dense rather than porous.   Porosity is therefore the reverse of plasticity and these two properties must be adjusted so as to balance each other.

The third necessary property is commonly known as vitrification but could be better named "densification" because complete vitrification is not attained in ordinary clay wares.   This property may be defined as that which causes a clay to yield to the action of a high temperature so that the result is a ware, more or less dense, which is hard, durable and sonorous.   With this there must be coupled a certain amount of resistance to heat treatment so that the pottery does not fuse or collapse during the firing.   Here also is found the need for adjustment. The clay must yield to the fire but not completely.   It must resist but not entirely.

Plasticity is due to the clay base.   Not only to its quantity but to its quality also.   Some forms of clay in which clay base predominates are not plastic because the clay base itself is coarse grained.   Other forms with less clay base present are plastic because this ingredient is fine grained and tough.   Pure clay base is also highly resistant to fire and therefore contributes to the refractoriness of the mass.

Porosity is caused by the sand in the clay.   Any kind of sand will produce porosity but the effect differs with the condition of the sand.   Coarse sand is more effective than fine sand. More sand will, of course, cause greater porosity.

Vitrification or densification is due to the feldspar or fusible sand. This also varies with the condition. A fine-grained feldspar will produce vitrification more easily than the same amount of coarse feldspar.

Certain substances are available for use in pottery mixtures, which possess one or other of the necessary properties in high degree so that they will impart these properties to a mass to which they are added.

Kaolin or china clay is usually fine, white, and refractory. Some kaolins are rather plastic but most of them are "short" in working and rather tender. For the production of a white ware kaolin is indispensable. No other ingredient will afford the pure white color which is sought after in porcelain and china.

Ball clay is very plastic, easily vitrified, but is not white. The color varies from a cream to a gray. The use of a ball clay is therefore limited in white wares because it will spoil the color. For wares in which a light cream color is not objectionable ball clays are valuable and almost indispensable.

Stoneware clay is usually a rather plastic clay which contains a good deal of sand, hence stoneware clays can be used for certain classes of ware without admixture. A rather high temperature is required for most of these clays, although occasionally one can be found that will become dense at the fire of a studio kiln.

Ground flint is a necessary ingredient in almost all pottery. It aids in the porosity of the clay and enables the mixture to be adjusted to fit a special glaze.

Ground feldspar is also necessary. Like flint it aids in

the porosity of the unburned clay but unlike flint it produces density in the firing.

By a proper adjustment of these ingredients a clay can be composed which will meet the special requirements of the worker.

In order to ascertain the properties of any given clay certain simple tests may be made and every clay worker should know how to do this because one cannot be too well informed as to the materials to be used.

First, water of plasticity. A certain portion of the clay, dried and powdered, is weighed out. It is convenient to weigh in grams and to measure in cubic centimeters because in this way calculation is easy. The scales and weights are described in the chapter on glazes. For measuring the water a glass vessel called a graduate is used. One holding 100 cubic centimeters and graduated in centimeters and tenths can be obtained from a dealer in chemical supplies. One hundred grams of clay is weighed out and transferred to a glass slab. The graduate is filled with water to the one-hundred mark. Some of this water is then poured on to the clay, adding little by little as needed until the whole can be worked into a stiff mass of the proper plasticity. The quantity of water used is then carefully noted by observing how much is left in the graduate. Suppose, for instance, 70 cubic centimeters remain. The hundred grams of clay have absorbed 30 cubic centimeters of water. Inasmuch as 1 cubic centimeter of water weighs 1 gram, the clay has taken just 30 per cent. This amount is important because it is one of the best indications of plasticity. A very plastic clay may need 40 per cent, a non-plastic clay may be satisfied with 25 per cent.

Second, shrinkage.   The mass of plastic clay is now transferred to a plaster bat and rolled or pressed out into a smooth slab about 12 centimeters long.   Here again the centimeter is used in preference to the inch as being more easily calculated.   A faint line is ruled on the clay slab and two fine scratches are marked exactly 10 centimeters apart.   The edges are trimmed and the excess clay made up into three or four small pieces which are to be fired in different parts of the kiln as tests for density. When the clay slab is dry the distance between the marks is measured and noted.   The 10 centimeters being divided into 100 millimeters, each millimeter of shrinkage means 1 per cent.   After firing, a second measurement is made and the differences are noted as dry shrinkage and fire shrinkage, respectively.

Third, firing.   The slab with the measurement upon it is set in the kiln in the place where the clay wares are to receive the first or biscuit fire and the small pieces are arranged in different places so as to secure as many different conditions as possible.   The position of each should be carefully recorded.   After firing, the marks on the slab are measured as already described and note is taken of any warping of the piece.   The color is also recorded. The small pieces should be tested for porosity or absorption of water but this is rather a delicate operation and needs a particularly sensitive balance.   Generally it will suffice to use a wet sponge or to dip each piece into water, removing it quickly and noting carefully the rate of speed at which the water is absorbed.   If the water should be scarcely absorbed at all a line of ink may be drawn upon the pottery with a pen, the piece being perfectly dry.   In a fully vitrified ware the ink can be washed off, leaving scarcely a mark but the test is quite sensitive and with a little practice will afford an excellent means of comparing the density of different clays or of the same clay at different temperatures.

Fourth, glazing.   It is well to have ready a small supply of a standard clear glaze.   Each of the test pieces should be covered with this in a rather thin coat and then they should all be fired again, this time close together so that they will receive the same heat treatment.   This will enable one to determine what degree of fire for the clay will best suit the glaze.

CHAPTER IV

THE PREPARATION OF THE CLAY

A CLAY having been selected in accordance with the tests described, it becomes necessary to prepare it for use. A fairly large supply should be obtained and stored in a dry place. Most natural clays need some kind of cleansing for there are almost always foreign substances present. This cleansing is accomplished by reducing the clay to the fluid known as slip. The necessary appliances for making slip are as follows:

A large sieve of quarter-inch mesh.

A small wire sieve of about 14 meshes to the inch.

A large barrel.

Two galvanized pails.

The clay is, after drying, powdered and sifted through the large sieve. One of the pails is half filled with clean water and the clay, handful by handful, is sprinkled into it. The clay rapidly absorbs the water and sinks to the bottom. The addition of clay is continued until a small mound rises through the water, when the whole is left to soak for an hour. The bared arm is then plunged into the pail and the mass stirred vigorously. A stick or paddle will serve, of course, but the potter learns a great deal by the feel of the clay and therefore the hand is best. It is said that he is a poor sailor who will not dip his hands in the tar bucket and, in like manner, he is a poor potter who fears the slip tub. This stirring will tell a good deal about the probable working of the clay. It may be stony or sandy or greasy. The large stones and roots will have been removed by the sieve but now, after thorough mixing, the slip is poured through the small sieve into the barrel.   Both pails may be kept going at once, one being filled while the other is soaking and so on until the barrel is full or, at least, a good quantity of slip has been prepared.

If the clay is very sandy, it should be washed.   The mixture in the pail, having been well stirred, is allowed to stand for a definite time, say 1 minute.   The slip is then poured into the second pail and it will be found that a quantity of sand has settled.   This is thrown away and the slip in the second pail is examined.   If enough sand has been removed, the slip may be poured into the barrel, using the fine sieve as already described.   If still sandy the process should be repeated, the settling time being 2 minutes.   Experience is the best guide in this operation but all the sand should not be removed.

When the barrel is full of slip it is allowed to stand overnight when some inches of clear water will be found at the top.   This is removed with a siphon which may be made of a piece of lead or rubber pipe.   The removal of the water results in the thickening of the slip and the contents of the barrel should be thoroughly stirred with a long wooden paddle to insure a uniform consistency.   If the slip is found to be still thin another settling and removal of the water will thicken it.

The slip thus prepared will keep indefinitely, provided that it is not allowed to become dry by evaporation.   It improves greatly with age.   This is the material which is used for casting, as will be described later, but for plastic work it must be thickened still more.   A shallow box may be procured and made watertight and the slip, when poured into it, will thicken much more rapidly than in the barrel, but it is better to have some shallow plaster dishes as the plaster itself absorbs the water and thickens the clay. Instructions for making these dishes appear in the chapter on plaster.

These directions will suffice for the preparation of a natural clay but it is sometimes desired to prepare a white body either of earthenware or porcelain. These bodies do not exist in nature and therefore a mixture must be made. The ingredients are kaolin or white porcelain clay, ball clay or plastic potters' clay, ground quartz or flint, and ground feldspar.

A suitable mixture for earthenware is—

Georgia Clay	20 parts by weight
Tennessee Ball Clay	30 parts by weight
Flint	35 parts by weight
Feldspar	15 parts by weight
	100

and for porcelain—

Georgia Clay	45 parts by weight
Flint	35 parts by weight
Feldspar	20 parts by weight
	100

The earthenware will be creamy in color and porous at an ordinary fire. The porcelain will need a hard fire and will be white and translucent. It is, however, non-plastic and hard to work. The preparation of these mixtures, of course, necessitates a pair of scales but otherwise the treatment of the mix is the same as that of natural clay. Washing is not necessary but the clay must be powdered, mixed with the flint and spar, and sprinkled into water as already described. In place of the wire sieve, however, a silk lawn of 120 meshes to the inch should be used.

The lawn is simply a fine sieve and is so named after the material (also called bolting cloth) with which it is covered. Have a carpenter make a box without a bottom. Cypress or oak should be used and this should be a full half inch thick. Four strips of the same thickness are also to be provided. The box may be of any convenient size; 8 inches square and 4 inches deep is about right. The sides should be fastened together with brass screws to avoid rust and a piece of lawn is strained tightly across the bottom and secured with copper or brass tacks. A strip of coarse muslin folded and laid along the edges will help to prevent the lawn from tearing, the tacks being, of course, driven through both muslin and lawn. Then the four wooden strips are set upon the muslin and secured with brass screws. The completed lawn is then a tray of which the bottom is formed of lawn. The strips of wood beneath serve to protect the lawn when placed on a table as well as to assist in holding it firmly.*

For storing clay in the plastic state there is nothing better than stoneware jars. These may be had of any size and a tinman should make close-fitting covers. Earthenware covers do not fit tight and are always getting broken. A little water is poured into each jar and a support provided for the clay so that it does not rest in contact with the water. Under any conditions clay will slowly harden so that not too large a stock should be kept. Slip, on the other hand, keeps well so long as some water is always on the top and it is not a long process to stiffen it into clay.

---

* Brass sieves ready for use from the W. S. Tyler Company, Cleveland, Ohio.

CHAPTER V

MOLD–MAKING AND PLASTER

PLASTER is almost a necessity to the potter and therefore something should be learned about it. Even if one does not use molds there are numberless purposes for which plaster is convenient. For stiffening slip into clay, and for absorbing water from glazes, shallow dishes of plaster are used, and for holding work either in making or drying, plaster bats or round slabs are always in demand.

It is best to purchase the finest quality of potters' plaster by the barrel. It will keep indefinitely if stored in a dry place. The necessary appliances are:

One or two large jugs for mixing, or a metal can with a spout.

A metal spider or frying pan.

Six feet of rubber machine belting, 6 inches wide, or similar strips cut from linoleum or enameled cloth.

Two or three thin pieces of steel of various degrees of flexibility (scrapers).

Handy knives, called vegetable knives.

A small sized painter's brush.

Two or three fine sponges.

To begin with, a size of soft soap and water is prepared. Put a quart of water into a kettle and add a piece of soap the size of an egg.* Simmer for an hour or until the soap is entirely dissolved and then set aside to cool.

* Any good laundry soap will serve, but it should be sliced thin.

When cold the size should be of the consistency of maple syrup. This size is used whenever plaster is to be kept from sticking to a form or surface, and it has also the merit of causing clay to stick to plaster. For example, if a mold is to be taken from a clay model no size should be used, but if a plaster form is used as a foundation for clay ornament it should be well sized first. The size is laid on with a brush and wiped off with a sponge. Another sponge is then used with clean water and the sized surface is washed, all superfluous water being removed. Size is then applied a second time and washed off as before. A third application is sometimes necessary, or until the sized surface rejects water like grease does. On the last sizing, water is not applied, but the surface is polished with the sponge containing size. If the surface to be prepared is of wood or metal, a single coat of size will often suffice; but if it is of plaster, three or four applications are often necessary.

The first lesson may well be the manufacture of a plaster bat. The frying pan is first sized and set upon a level table. Let us suppose that a quart of water covers the pan to a depth of about 1 inch. This amount of water is put into a jug and 2¾ pounds of dry plaster are weighed out and allowed to trickle through the fingers into the water. This proportion has been found to be best for ordinary mixings. A smaller quantity of plaster to the quart of water will result in a very soft bat; a larger quantity will be proportionately harder. After the plaster has soaked up all the water it will take in about 2 minutes' time, the hand is plunged in and the mass stirred to a smooth cream. All lumps must be broken up and the air bubbles removed as far as possible. Continue stirring gently and presently the mixture will be felt to grow thicker. The psychological moment arrives when the plaster forms on the hand a white coating which cannot be shaken off. The creamy liquid is then poured into the frying pan which is shaken gently to level the surface.

If the plaster has been poured at the right moment it will set smoothly with a mat surface like sugar icing. If poured too late it will be stiff and difficult to level, and if poured too soon it will curdle on the surface and water will be seen above the plaster. A little practice will show

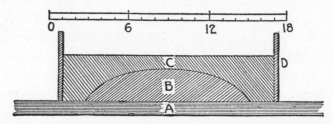

Fig. 1. *A*, table. *B*, clay mound. *C*, plaster. *D*, rubber belt.

the right moment. The jug should be washed out immediately while the plaster is soft. In the place used for plaster work a tub should be provided in which all vessels and tools can be washed, for, if allowed to flow down the waste pipe of a sink, the plaster will speedily choke the outflow.

After standing for some 10 minutes, more or less, the bat in the frying pan will grow warm. This is the sign of a combination between the plaster and the water and shows the completion of the setting. The pan is now taken by the handle and, holding it upside down, the edge is rapped smartly on a brick or stone. This will cause the contents to fall out in the form of a smooth disk which is one of the most useful of appliances. The edge will need to be scraped and the bat can be set aside until needed. It will be good practice to make a half dozen of these.

This process of mixing and pouring plaster is the same for all operations and the instructions will not be repeated, but when the student is told to "pour plaster" it will be presumed that this experiment has already been made.

The next step is the making of a plaster bowl or dish for the purpose of drying out slip or glaze. A convenient size should be decided upon as it is best to have all the dishes the same. Upon any flat, smooth surface a mound of clay is reared which shall be the size and depth of the inside of the proposed dish. About 12 inches in diameter and 3 inches deep is a good size, although 14 inches is not too large for the diameter. This mound should be made as nearly circular as possible and the clay finished to a smooth consistency. The rubber belt is then set around the mound in the form of a hoop leaving a space of 2 inches between the clay mound and the rubber hoop. The rubber is fastened either by tying with string or by binding the overlapping ends with clothes pins. A roll of soft clay is laid down where the belt joins the table and is pressed down outside to prevent leakage. Enough plaster to fill the space within the belt is now mixed and poured, covering the clay mound to a depth of at least 1 inch. When the plaster has set the rubber is detached, the whole turned over and the clay dug out. We have now a circular plaster dish 3 inches deep, but we have only one. The trouble of rebuilding the clay is unnecessary a second time because a "case" or reverse can be made from which as many dishes as may be necessary can be formed.

The dish is carefully smoothed and trimmed. The sharp edge is removed and the inside is dressed with fine sandpaper to a perfectly smooth surface. Size is now applied to the inside and upper edge until a bright slippery

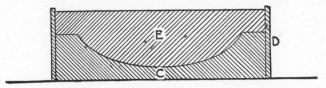

Fig. 2.   C, plaster dish.   D, rubber belt.   E, plaster case or reverse.

surface is obtained. The rubber belt is now bound closely around the dish and plaster is poured to a depth of about 1½ inches on the edge. This, of course, makes a depth of 4½ inches in the center. When this new plaster

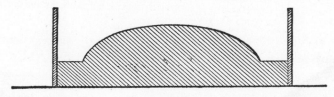

Fig. 3.   Plaster case, with rubber belt, arranged for pouring.

has set in turn the rubber is removed and the two castings can be easily separated by inserting a knife at the junction. The knife should be gently driven in with a hamber. Obviously it is now possible to make a number of dishes from the reverse thus obtained, by simply binding the rubber belt around each time and pouring plaster as at first. The original mold having been sized is no longer absorbent but must be kept in case additional reverses are needed. The molds or dishes must be thoroughly dried out before being used.

The molding of a vase form is more elaborate but not really difficult. Even if one does not intend to produce pottery by molding there is always an advantage in having a number of simple forms upon which to make experiments.

The vase to be molded is first drawn to exact size upon paper and a plaster model is turned on a lathe. This can be done equally well on the potters' wheel and the

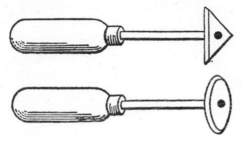

FIG. 4. Turning tools for plaster.

method is as follows: A plaster bat is saturated with water and set upon the wheel so as to run true when the wheel is revolved, and is cemented to the wheel head by a little slip. A few deep scratches are made on the face of the bat and a cylinder, either of the rubber belt or of stiff paper, is rolled up and set on end in the center of the bat. The size of the cylinder should be a little larger every way than the proposed vase. Plaster is now mixed and poured to fill the cylinder. It will adhere to the bat below by reason of the scratches. When the plaster has set, the cylinder is unfastened and removed and the turning may begin. To turn plaster well involves a good deal of practice but it is better to spoil three or four plaster cores in the learning than to spend a long time on one for fear of damaging it.

The board support and turning stick described on page 69 are used in turning plaster as well as clay. The turning stick is held in the left hand and the point is pressed into the board. All this, of course, is made ready before the plaster is poured. The turning tools are shown in

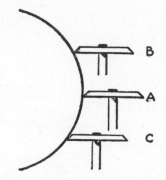

FIG. 5. Position of tool in turning.
A, correct. *B* and *C*, incorrect.

Fig. 4. They are not sold in the stores but can be made by any machinist. The head or cutting blade consists of a flat piece of steel through the center of which is a shaft or pin which is driven into a handle. The head may be of any shape but the triangle and the circle will meet every need. The tool is held in the right hand and braced against the turning stick, the stick and tool being moved together by raising or lowering the left hand which holds the butt of the stick.

While the plaster is still soft the round tool is used and the rough form is rapidly turned. Then as the setting of the plaster proceeds and it is found to grow harder, the triangle tool should be used and the shape gradually wrought out with the point. Finally by using the circle tool for concave lines the form is perfected. The surface is to be finished and the tool marks removed by using, free hand, a flexible scraper which is bent by the fingers and thumb to fit the lines of the form, and a final smooth-

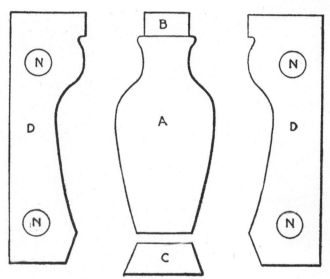

FIG. 6. Vase with foot piece and template. *A*, vase. *B*, spare. *C*, foot piece. *D D*, templates. *N N N N*, natches.

ing is given by fine sandpaper, the wheel being revolved all the time. At the top of the form a small cylindrical piece is left, called the "spare" which represents the thickness of the mold substance, and for the bottom a small piece is turned in the shape of a truncated cone. The small end of this should be the same diameter as the base of the vase. These are shown in Fig. 6.

It will be obvious that in the directions given above the base of the vase is not finished off and therefore the form must be cut off from the bat, either by a knife or saw, and the base is then finished by hand, or by setting the form upside down in a clay cradle—called a "chum"—and turning the base true. The form is now ready for molding.

The plaster vase is laid upon its side on a piece of soft clay and a thin bat or plaster slab is cut to fit the outline.

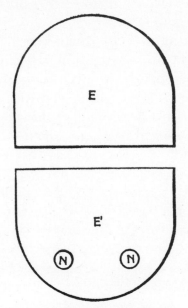

FIG. 7. End plates for mold.
E, upper plate.
E', lower plate.
N N, natches.

This template should fit with reasonable accuracy but need not be absolutely exact. A pair of these will be required, one to fit each side of the form. These slabs or sheets of plaster are always useful and if a sheet of glass is kept handy any excess of plaster left from a mixing may be poured on to it. After setting, this is easily detached and will present a smooth face where it has rested on the glass. The pair of templates must include, in their outline, both the spare and the foot piece but should not extend beyond either of these. The outside diameter of the mold is now to be determined and the templates cut to this dimension so that the two together, with the vase between them, constitute a longitudinal section of the mold.

The vase must now be divided accurately into two halves by a line running from top to bottom. There are several ways of doing this. While the form is still on the bat a diameter of the bat may be drawn and a perpendicular erected from each end of this diameter. These perpendicular lines will, of course, mark the center of the vase on each side; or after the vase has been cut off another method is possible. With a pair of dividers find the center of both the top and the bottom of the vase. Mark each with a small hole or the point of a pencil. Now lay the vase on its side on the clay cradle upon a glass sheet or other level surface and raise or depress one end until the two centers are exactly the same height from the glass. Take this height in the dividers and, sliding one of the compass legs along the glass, gently scratch the plaster vase with the other or upper point. If the two centers have been accurately adjusted this scratch line will be the exact center of the form.

Some soft clay is now built up on each side of the vase and the templates are pressed down upon it, one on each side until the upper face of each corresponds with the scratched line. The vase is now seen to be half buried in a plaster surface, and plaster poured on this will give a half mold. There is yet, however, nothing to confine the plaster and it would flow away as fast as poured. Two end plates are necessary and these must rise in a half circle above the bed formed by the templates. The part below may be of any shape but must be high enough to cause the diameter of the half circle to coincide with the plane of the templates. Two pieces of cardboard, wood, or rubber belt are now bound to the sides, the apertures at the top and bottom, caused by the curve of the end plates, are stopped with clay and the whole presents the appearance of a vase, only half of which is visible, lying in a shallow trough. All the fitting should be carefully done but the tying up is not yet. The whole is now taken apart and well sized. Vase, foot piece, templates and end pieces are all to be sized thoroughly in the manner described. They are then put together again and bound around with twine. It is necessary now to make provision for the proper fitting of the halves of the mold. This is done by providing knobs and hollows which fit together. These are technically known as "natches" and will be referred to as such. Take two pieces of moderately stiff clay each about the size of a cherry. Roll them into neat balls and cut them in two with a thin knife. Lay each of the halves, flat side down, upon the templates, two on each, placing them in pairs opposite to each other. Affix two or more of these on the inner face of the bottom end plate. Now mix and pour the plaster. This should be poured to the height of the top of the end plates and, after pouring, shake this well down by dipping the fingers into it, so that no bubbles may cling to the surfaces below. As soon as the plaster has become firm but while it is still soft remove the string and the side boards, pull off the pieces of clay and with a straight, thin piece of wood scrape off the surplus of plaster by following the line of the end plates and thus making a half cylinder.

As soon as the plaster has become warm the whole may be turned over and the templates and end plates removed. The four half spheres of clay will be found embedded in the face of the plaster and these, being removed, will leave four hemispherical depressions. The vase can now be gently detached from its bed and the first half of the mold completed. A little dressing will be necessary. All overhanging edges and rough places should be finished off and the hollow natches smoothed with a piece of muslin on the end of a finger.

The second half is simple. Replace the vase in the half mold, set the foot piece in its place, replace the end plates with the diameter on the line as before but with the semicircular edges upward, and set two or three clay natches on the bottom one. Size, bind up, pour and scrape off as before, thus completing the two halves of the mold in cylindrical form. It only now remains to make the bottom for, at present, the mold is open at both ends.

The two halves with the vase inside are bound very tightly together with twine and set on the table, bottom upward. The clay natches in the bottom are taken out and the hollows smoothed. The foot piece is taken out and the rough places dressed. The bottom end of the vase is now visible and this, together with the end of the mold, is sized. A strip of stout paper is bound around the mold, projecting about an inch above the end and plaster is poured to fill it. When this is set the paper is peeled off and the edges of the mold are dressed smooth.

The bottom may now be detached by inserting a thin knife at the junction, the mold opened and the form taken out. The mold is now in three parts which may be put together at will and used for casting the vase in clay.

Chapter VI

CASES AND WORKING MOLDS

THE mold described in the previous chapter is called, technically, a "block mold" and is not, as a rule, used for making the clay ware. The reason for this is that molds wear out more or less rapidly, and to repeat the process of making new ones from the original form would be tedious and expensive.

From the block mold a reverse is made, called a "case," and from this, in turn, working molds are made in any required number. While it is possible to use the block mold as a working mold, and, if only a few pieces are required this is quite sufficient, yet, as it is often necessary to have a number of molds, the student should understand how to make a case.

A case may be defined as a mold from which a mold is made. If one can imagine the visible half of the vase form as it appears in making the mold, with the templates and ends cemented into one piece, one has a conception of one half of a case. The problem is to make this with permanent but movable ends so as to have a convenient form from which half molds may be easily made.

The ends are joined to the body by means of offsets and the first step is the construction of these. One half of the block is taken and laid upon its back, being supported by clay so that the face is level and steady. An offset plate is now cut to fit each end. To make these a piece of plaster is selected or made which is true and smooth on both sides. The plates are cut of the same

41

width as the mold and are beveled at the upper edge so as to rise slightly from the mold face. The curve at the end of the mold is cut out to fit and beveled in like manner. Then two end plates are fitted. These should be about 2 inches higher than the offset plates and are

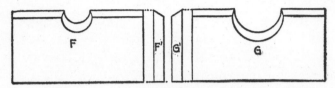

FIG. 8.   Offset plates.   *F*, top plate, front view.   *F'*, side view.
G G', bottom plate.

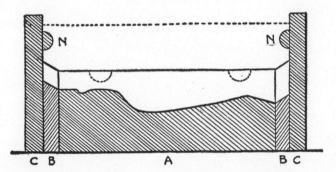

FIG. 9.   Sectional view of mold ready for casing.   *A*, mold.
B B, offset plates.   *C C*, end plates.   *N N*, natches.

square at the top. Upon each of these, two or three clay natches are set, being placed low down near the face of the mold. The mold and plates are well sized and bound together with side walls just as in the making of the mold. Plaster is poured to a height sufficient to well cover the natches and left to set hard. No shaping is necessary. When well set the end plates and offset plates are removed but the vase mold and the case are left attached. The other half of the mold is prepared and run in the same way, the same offset plates and end plates being used with such slight refitting as may be necessary. The work is now examined and all rough places and scraps of adhering plaster are removed. The two halves of the case, the half molds being still attached, are set up

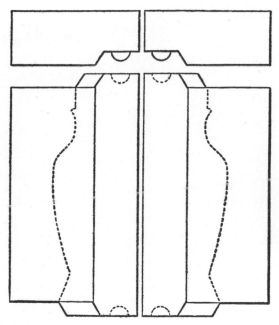

Fig. 10. Mold and case in position. The top ends are lifted to show fitting. The bottom ends are not shown.

on end, back to back, being separated by a thin piece of plaster or a strip of cardboard which should extend 2 inches above the top. The top ends are now sized, the natch holes having been smoothed off, a band of paper is tied around and plaster poured on top to a depth of about 1 inch. When set, the whole is turned over and the operation is repeated on the other end. After the final setting the ends are easily removed and by the insertion of a thin knife driven by a light blow, the molds and case are separated. Each half case is now laid on its back and the proper ends are fitted in place. It only now needs the usual side walls to be tied on and molds can be made with ease just as the original block mold was made.

It now remains to make a case of the bottom mold. The bottom piece of the block mold is taken and sized and with a strip of paper bound around it, plaster is

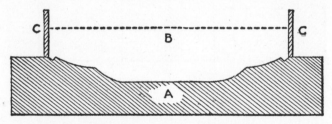

FIG. 11. Block of plaster with face of plate turned. *B*, height of plaster to be poured. *C*, rubber belt.

poured. The two are detached when set and the case is finished. It consists of seven pieces; three are used in each half and one for the bottom.

Thus equipped it is possible to make any number of working molds and if the case should wear out or be damaged, a new one can always be made from the block mold. The block mold itself, having been sized, is no longer absorbent and cannot be used for making vases. The working molds should be thoroughly dried before using and they will last longer.

Flat ware, such as plates and saucers, is made on, not in, a mold. The diameter of the plate having been decided, a block of plaster 3 inches wider is run. This is placed on the center of the wheel or jigger and in it the face of the plate is turned.   This must be sunk below the level of the block and, when finished, must appear as though the plate itself were embedded in the plaster. One half the thickness of the edge is shown in such a way that there is no under cutting.   Just outside of this edge the plaster is turned so as to slope gently up to the level of the block.

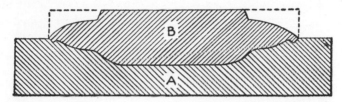

Fig. 12.   *A*, block of plaster.   *B*, mold poured on face of plate and turned.

Without removing the block from the wheel the face of the plate is well sized, a band of belting is arranged, of the same diameter as the edge of the slope, and plaster is poured to a depth of 3 inches.   Out of this the back of the mold is turned as shown in Fig. 12.

The top of this, as it lies upside down, is shaped with a straight, almost upright slope which enables the mold to be set securely in the wheel head.   Around the exposed edge of the original block, three or four natches are now bored or cut.   They should be placed at irregular distances so that there will be no doubt as to the putting together of the sides of the case.   If two circular pieces of plaster have to be set together and held by natches there should always be either this irregular spacing or some distinctive mark, because if this be not provided for, two or three trials will always be made before the correct fitting is found and these trials wear out the natches very quickly.

The back of the plate mold and the edges of the block are now sized and plaster is run to the level of the highest part of the mold but no higher (Fig. 13). When this is

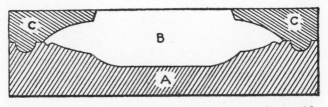

FIG. 13.   *A*, bottom of case.   *B*, cavity for pouring molds.
C, top of case.

set, the two halves of the case can be separated and the mold taken out. Now when the halves of the case are fitted together there will be a cavity the exact size of the

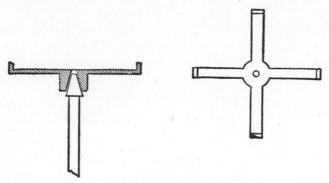

FIG. 14.   Iron prong to fit wheel head.

mold. This can be filled again and again with plaster, a new mold being formed each time.

In order to use these molds a special head must be provided for the wheel. The regular head of the wheel should be detachable and in its place an iron frame called a prong is fitted. This consists of a collar either with a hollow cone or a screw to fit the shaft of the wheel, and from this radiate four short arms. In order to use this a circular block of plaster some 2 or 3 inches thick is poured on a table or slab and just as this is setting, the

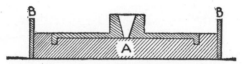

FIG. 15. *A*, plaster, with prong inserted.
B, rubber belt.

prong, upside down, is pressed into it just below the surface and held there until the plaster is hard enough to support the weight of the iron. When hard, the whole is lifted and the prong with the plaster attached is set in position on the wheel. This now forms a rough plaster

FIG. 16. Wheel head with plate mold. The tool used is shown in dotted outline.

head and it must be turned true. In this head a circular depression is to be turned which will exactly fit the back of the plate molds. If the recess should wear larger as it will if much used, a new head can be run easily. The same principle can be applied to the making of molds for saucers.

Cups and bowls are molded from the outside. A block of plaster about 1 inch thicker than the height of the proposed cup is taken and centered upon the wheel. Out of this the piece is to be turned, upside down, leaving a ledge or platform, the outside diameter of which is the size of the mold. The rubber belt is tied around this and the mold poured. If for casting this will suffice, but if it is intended to make the cups upon the wheel the outside of the mold must be turned to fit a wheel-head which is hollowed to receive it. The making of the cups is described in Chapter X. A bowl is simply an enlarged cup.

Chapter VII

BUILDING BY HAND

THE production of pottery by hand is a form of modeling but with the important difference that, while pieces modeled by art-school methods are not intended to be preserved in the clay itself, built pieces are destined for the fire. It is therefore necessary not only that a special clay be used but that the work be such as will hold under the strain of the burn. The composition of the clay has been dealt with in another chapter and it is presumed that the worker has decided upon the proper mix or has procured a suitable clay.

The charm of built ware lies in the subtle plastic quality which belongs to no other material or method. The work may be done with coils, with slabs, or by the addition of small pieces of clay worked to an even thickness with the fingers. Very large pieces such as tree pots may be built on the wheel and kept true as the work proceeds. Then a slight turning at the finish, when the clay is leather-hard, will produce a satisfactory result.

The clay for building should be rather soft as it is apt to dry quickly on handling. The work may be done either with coils or pieces.

A plaster bat should be made with a low dome in the center. This bat may either fit the wheel or not, depending upon the plan adopted. The dome is to raise up the bottom of the vase and form a foot. The table may be covered with a piece of oil cloth or may be kept slightly damp. The first attempt should be to build a cylinder as this form is easy to construct and to keep true, so that the attention may be devoted to the manipulation of the clay.

It is first necessary to roll out the clay into cords which should be a little thicker than the proposed walls are to be. These cords should be as uniform as possible and should be rolled quickly to avoid undue hardening. It is best to roll them as required. The domed bat is made quite damp and upon it should be marked the diameter of the cylinder to be built. A roll of clay is taken, one end laid in the center of the bat and the rest is coiled around it in a spiral line. When the disk so formed has reached the proper size, the coils are gently rubbed over with the fingers until they have thoroughly united and the lines of the spiral have disappeared. The clay disk may now be turned over and the rubbing continued on the other side. The circle is cut true and a new coil is laid on the outer edge thus making a shallow circular tray. In raising the walls it is best to pinch off the roll of clay when one circle has been completed and the new roll should be begun at another point so that all the joints will not be at the same place. This plan is better than coiling a long roll in a spiral for in this case one side of the piece will be higher than the other.

After three rolls have been laid in position the wall, both inside and out, should be worked like the bottom so that the rolls will disappear and the clay be welded uniformly together. This should be done without water or with as little as possible. The use of water is very tempting. It makes the clay so smooth and seems to help but it will inevitably make the work sloppy and will tend to soften the walls.

After three or four rolls have been worked in, the piece should be laid aside for some hours to stiffen. If this is not done the weight of the second building will cause the work to sag and fall out of shape. For this reason it is well to have two or three pieces in hand at once so that no waiting will be necessary. When the cylinder is of sufficient height it should be allowed to become quite stiff and then the irregularities should be corrected with a little soft clay which is worked into the joints. The whole surface may now be gone over with tools and brought to the required finish. As soon as the clay is hard enough it should be removed from the damp bat and placed upon a dry one to become dry.

In the method of building by pieces no rolls are prepared but the clay is taken, pinch by pinch, each morsel being pressed into place as the work goes on. This plan is somewhat more plastic in effect and is well adapted to free-hand work; the resulting pottery, however, is generally thicker and heavier.

The craft of building is not mastered until the lines of a drawing can be successfully followed. The clay is apt to choose its own way and the result will be very different from what the potter intended. The design should be carefully worked out on paper, full size if possible, and the clay form should be compared with the drawing as the building goes on. A profile may be cut in cardboard and this, applied to the clay from time to time, will verify the line, but all such mechanical aids should be used sparingly as the value of this work depends largely upon the sense of freedom and self-expression which belongs to it.

The thickness of the clay walls is a matter of great importance. A small piece should not be so thick as to feel clumsy and heavy, nor should a large piece be so thin as to lose the sense of strength and solidity.

Upon drying the ware, cracks may develop, especially in the bottom. The cause may be in the clay. A clay which is too plastic or too fine in the grain will surely crack. Such a clay may be opened or meagered by the addition of ground flint or fine grog. The cause may, on the other hand, be in the building. If the welding of the coils or pieces is imperfect, cracks are sure to result. If the bottom is too thick it will crack. A great strain is put upon the bottom in drying. The clay must be able to shrink and while the side walls are able to settle down on themselves, the bottom is pulled in every direction by the sides. The bottom should be made quite thin in the center and thicker toward the edges. This will help to avoid cracks. A bad crack cannot be successfully mended. It is best to break the piece and begin again. To burn it means the loss of the clay but the clay will be saved if the damaged work is withheld from the kiln. A small crack on the edge is also hopeless. A crack showing on the edge of a piece is a bad fault. A small crack in the bottom may be mended by dampening the place carefully and pressing in a little stiff clay.

Chapter VIII

THE POTTER'S WHEEL

MUCH of the glamour of the potter's art is associated with the wheel. Poets have sung its praise and artists have delighted in its rhythmic motion, but alas! the wheel as a commercial method of manufacture is doomed to extinction. It cannot compete with the precision and speed of machinery. It devolves, therefore, upon the artist potter to maintain the wheel in its rightful place as, *par excellence,* the potter's tool.

No clay worker's studio should be without a wheel, but the particular form of wheel depends upon the nature of the circumstances under which it is to be employed.

The simplest wheel is that used by the Chinese. A circular plate with a heavy rim is set upon a spindle so that it will revolve freely and run steadily. As the workman sits or kneels upon the floor the surface of the wheel is about at the floor level. Around the periphery and upon the upper surface four holes are sunk and the workman, inserting a short stick into one of these, gives the wheel a rapid motion. Then while it is revolving by its own momentum the clay is centered and shaped. As the motion is lost the stick is again inserted and the wheel spun. This method, of course, involves much skill on the part of the workman.

In the next form, one which is only adapted, however, for crude experimental work, the wheel is set upon the frame of a sewing machine and operated by the treadle.

A beginning may be made upon such a wheel but the operator will soon wish for something better.

A common factory form and one which is well adapted for studio work is the kick wheel. The wheel head is set at the top of a spindle and in the upright shaft there is a crank to which is attached a horizontal moving treadle. This is worked continuously by the left foot, the weight of the body being supported by the right. The action is strenuous and scarcely fitted for persons of other than robust physique but it can be used successfully after practice. This wheel is made by the manufacturers of potter's machinery.

Another form of the kick wheel is used in Europe and is, in fact, the original wheel used by the French and German potters in the seventeenth century. The head is set on a spindle as usual but, instead of the crank, there is a large, heavy disk on the bottom of the shaft which revolves in a horizontal plane. This is within reach of the foot and the operator, being seated, imparts a rapid motion by pushing. usually with the ball of the right toe. The momentum is kept up by the weight of the disk and there is a great advantage in that the foot need not be in continuous motion. On the other hand, it is difficult to acquire sufficient speed and power for the work.

There are several forms of machine wheels which are entirely satisfactory but which need the application of power. If a gas engine or a water motor or electric current is available, every effort should be made to obtain a wheel of this description. The prime motion is imparted to a short horizontal shaft which moves at a constant speed. Then the operator, seated in comfort, regulates the speed of the wheel itself by pressure upon a treadle. No action is required but a simple pressure, light for a slow speed and heavy for rapidity. Where the electric current is available, nothing could be better. Self-contained motor-driven wheels are available but are rather expensive.

One more plan may be mentioned in which the wheel is simply a vertical lathe with a belt and handle to be turned by an assistant. This may be convenient for some but it is not always possible to secure help at the moment when the wheel is to be used. Moreover the cost of labor would soon pay for a mechanical wheel.*

Whatever type of wheel is selected it should be arranged with a head which can be removed. There are two methods of constructing this: the head may be screwed on to the spindle, or the latter may terminate in a cone-shaped plug upon which the wheel head is made to fit, as shown in Fig. 14. The latter plan is to be preferred as the head can be removed more quickly and is not so likely to work loose. Several heads for the wheel can then be provided, one for regular work, one for making plates, one for finishing, etc.

The regular operation performed upon the wheel is termed either throwing or turning according to the industry in which it is employed, but in this description the word "throwing" will be used because the subsequent operation in which tools are employed is best described as turning.

The best head for the wheel to be used in throwing is made of hard wood or brass because the ball of clay can

---

* Information as to the usual types of wheel may be obtained from The Crossley Manufacturing Company, Trenton, N. J.; The Patterson Foundry and Machine Company, East Liverpool, Ohio; a wheel operated like a sewing machine is sold by the Lewis Institute, Chicago.

be easily centered upon a smooth surface. This, however, involves that the work shall be cut off with a wire and removed while soft. This is commonly done by professionals but is beyond the skill of the beginner. It is best, therefore, to use a head like that illustrated for plate making and to have a number of specially shaped plaster bats to fit the recess (Fig. 17). Then when the piece is formed, the bat with its burden can be set aside for the work to harden.

Throwing is not an easy operation to describe but the following instructions in the form of lessons will, with a large amount of practice, enable the student to become fairly expert. Every opportunity should be taken to

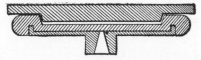

Fig. 17.   Wheel head with detached bat.

watch a good potter at work. There are a thousand and one little tricks in the position of the arms, hands, thumbs and fingers which are impossible to describe but which can be copied easily. If a kick wheel is used some time must be given to practicing the motion without using clay. The action of the foot must become subconscious or automatic like the pedaling of a bicycle, so that simply to will a change of speed is to accomplish it.

Lesson I.   Take the bat about to be used, plunge it in clean water and soak it nearly, but not quite, to saturation. If the bat remains wet 1 minute after being taken from the water it has soaked too long and must be dried off a little. A wet bat causes the clay to slip so that it cannot be held in one place. The proper dampness is secured when the clay ball can be pushed along the surface of the bat but does not slip easily. This condition is important and should be secured by experiment, because, if not right, good work will be impossible.

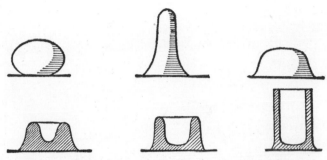

Fig. 18. The progress of a clay ball on the wheel.

Lesson II. Place a small basin of water close at hand. Take a ball of clay about 3 inches in diameter. Set it on the center of the wheel as nearly as can be judged. Now spin the wheel at a fairly rapid rate. Brace the left elbow against the side and, wetting the hand, press the ball of the thumb and the lower part of the palm against the clay. The left forearm being kept rigid, the clay as it revolves will be forced into the center of the wheel. Use the right hand to sprinkle water on the clay so that proper lubrication may be maintained. With the fingers of the right hand pull the clay toward you, at the same time pressing inward with left hand and so squeezing the clay. As the hands come together the clay will rise in a cone. Do not pull it upward but let it rise as it is squeezed. Now bring the hands over the top and with the thumbs together press down again. Lumps and irregularities will be felt in the clay and the operations of spinning up and pressing down must be continued until

PLATE I.   Throwing.—Lesson II, 1.

PLATE II.   Throwing.—Lesson II, 2.

58

PLATE III. THROWING.—LESSON II, 3.

PLATE IV. THROWING.—LESSON III, 1.

these disappear.   Repeat the exercise of centering with a fresh ball of clay until it can be accomplished with ease and rapidity.   The clay so used is not wasted.   The superfluous water may be dried off upon a plaster bat and the clay wedged up for use again.

This wedging or waging of clay—the word has descended from the old English potters—is important.   A strong table should be built of which the top, measuring about 30 by 20 inches, is made of 2-inch plank.   A raised edge 2 inches high is fastened firmly by being nailed to the sides; the trough thus formed is then filled with plaster and allowed to harden.   An upright post is fastened in the center of one side and from the top of this a fine brass wire is stretched to the other side of the table, thus making a diagonal.   The worker stands at the side of the table opposite the post.   The ball of clay is taken in both hands and cut in two against the wire, then the pieces are slapped smartly upon the plaster, one on top of the other. The whole lump is then lifted, cut in two and slapped down as before.   The lump of clay is thus formed into layers, the irregularities in hardness are corrected and the clay made smooth.   A little practice will make the work quite easy but it will often be found necessary to cut and beat the clay fifteen or twenty times before a good texture is secured.   If the plaster table is dry the clay will be stiffened rapidly, but the plaster may be made wet to prevent this if it should be necessary.   A clay may also be softened in this way by sprinkling it with water as the wedging goes on.

Lesson III.   Center the ball as in Lesson II and moisten both hands and the clay.   Grasping the clay lightly but with sufficient force, press the right thumb down-

PLATE V. THROWING.—LESSON III, 2.

PLATE VI. THROWING.—LESSON IV, 1.

ward and toward the palm, thus forming a cup-shaped hollow in the clay. Raise the right hand slowly, still keeping a light pressure upon the clay with the thumb. The clay wall will rise with the hand. Now insert the two first fingers of the left hand into the hollow and hold them against the right-hand wall. Slacken the speed of the wheel a little. Bend the forefinger of the right hand and press the second joint and the knuckle against the outer wall so as to oppose the fingers which are inside. Press the thumbs together to steady the hands and raise both hands upward together. The fingers inside and outside the clay should be kept at a definite distance apart so that, as the hands rise, the clay is brought to a uniform thickness. The hands are brought steadily to the full height to which the clay will go and thus a cylinder is formed.

Repeat this lesson three or four times with fresh clay.

Lesson IV. Keep the hands wet. Shape the clay cylinder as directed in the previous exercise. Now repeat the action of the fingers inside and outside and, beginning at the bottom, take a closer grip of the clay and draw up the walls as before. The cylinder is now taller and the walls thinner. Do this again and again taking a little closer grip each time until the cylinder is as tall and as thin as the clay will bear. The walls will probably spread as the work proceeds and the hands must then be used outside. Grasp the clay with both hands and squeeze it slightly; at the same time raise the hands upward. This will reduce the diameter of the cylinder and thicken the walls. The operation of the fingers can then be repeated until the full height is reached. There is, of course, a limit to the height of the cylinder which can

PLATE VII.   THROWING.—LESSON IV, 2.

PLATE VIII.   THROWING.—LESSON V.

be made from a given lump of clay and it is best to begin on a small scale. A ball of clay which can be easily grasped with the hands is the proper size with which to learn. A very small ball is nearly as hard to work as a large one. Repeat this lesson until a tall cylinder can be made with ease and certainty.

Lesson V. Keep the hands wet. Spin up a cylinder with thick walls as in Lesson III. With the fingers of the one hand inside and those of the other hand outside, open the cylinder gradually. Keep the wheel at a slow speed. If the edge runs unevenly, use both hands outside to steady it, then work outward again until a shallow bowl is formed.

Lesson VI. Keep the hands wet. Spin up a cylinder of medium height as in Lesson IV. With the fingers of the right hand outside press inward at the base of the cylinder close to the bat and with the fingers of the left hand inside, press outward at a slightly higher level. This will reduce the diameter at the bottom and increase it in the middle, making a cup shape. Now raise the right hand and gently draw the top inward. With the left hand inside press the upper edge outward and with the fingers of the right hand shape the upper part into the form of a jar or flower pot.

Lesson VII. Keep the hands wet; proceed as in Lesson VI. Instead of making the top flange outward, draw it gradually inward into a globe form. Work the clay carefully upward and inward until the opening at the top is almost closed. Several attempts will probably have to be made before this result can be secured.

Lesson VIII. Keep the hands wet. Spin up a globe shape with a narrow base as in Lesson VI but carry a good

PLATE IX.   THROWING.—LESSON VI, 1.

PLATE X.   THROWING.—LESSON VI, 2.

PLATE XI.   THROWING.—LESSON VII.

PLATE XII.   THROWING.—LESSON VIII, 1.

66

PLATE XIII. THROWING.—LESSON VIII, 2.

share of the clay to the top so that the upper edge of the globe is quite thick. Insert two fingers of the left hand and with the fingers of the right hand outside work the upper edge of the globe into a tall neck. The action is the same as in the shaping of a cylinder except that the diameter is smaller. A good deal of practice will be necessary in order to keep the neck thin and to raise it to any appreciable height, but perseverance will master it.

These lessons, if carried out conscientiously, will enable the operator to produce almost any form in so far as the manipulation of the clay is concerned but the work up to this point is drill only. It is not intended that the pieces should be preserved. The next point is to insist that the clay obey the potter in the shaping of a form.

A simple drawing of a jar should be made exact to the size proposed. Two or three pairs of calipers are provided and with them the diameter of each part of the drawing is taken. Of course a single pair could be made to serve, but it is very inconvenient to change measurements while working. A piece of wood also is cut to the height of the proposed piece. The throwing is begun as usual by making a cylinder. This should be higher than the drawing for the clay sinks in the shaping. First the bottom is pressed into the proper size (Lesson VI). Then the body is enlarged to the required measure and, lastly, the diameter of the top is taken and the height brought to the determined point. If too high the superfluous clay may be cut off with a pointed knife, the edge being carefully rounded afterward.

It is only by checking up one's work in some such way as this that real power can be acquired. The skilled worker can think in the clay and create forms at will upon the moving wheel, but for the beginner to attempt this is like an endeavor to paint pictures before one has learned to draw. Shape after shape should be designed, drawn to scale and thrown to measure; in fact, for elaborate pieces no other course is possible.

Chapter IX

TURNING

IT is not possible to finish work to perfection in the operation of throwing. The clay is too soft to handle and for proper finishing the piece must be turned over to get at the bottom. An experienced thrower reduces the final work to a minimum and this, of course, is the ideal plan. Even in factory practice every thrown piece is passed on to the turner so that the phrase "thrown and turned" is used as of a single operation, even though, in fact, it expresses not only two processes but the work of two men.

The artist-potter, therefore, must learn to turn, although this process should not be overemphasized. Many persons, in the pride of having produced some sort of a form on the wheel, will leave it in the crudest possible condition and trust to the turning tool to remove defects. If the lessons on throwing have been conscientiously carried out, this error will not be committed.

A half-dozen cylinders of convenient size should be thrown on separate bats and set aside in a cool place to harden. They must not be dried but should be in the condition known as "leather hard." If thrown one day they will be ready for turning the next morning. Pieces thus hardened are no longer flexible. They can be handled freely and the clay can be easily cut with a knife.

The equipment for turning consists of a board support, a turning stick and a set of tools. The board is of soft pine, 8 or 10 inches wide and 2 feet high and is set

upright at the back of the wheel frame opposite the workman.   It may be screwed in position if it does not interfere with the throwing, or it may be set in a socket so as
to be removed when not in use.   Its purpose is to support the end of the turning stick.   The stick is an ordinary broomstick in the end of which is a sharpened nail.

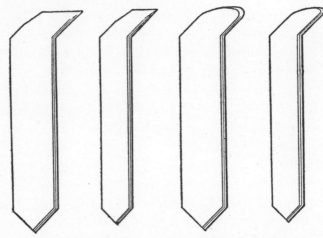

FIG. 19.   Turning tools bent and sharpened.

In use the end of the stick is held in the left hand and the
point is pressed into the board at any required height.
The right hand, holding the tool, is rested on the stick
just as the hand of a painter rests on the mahl-stick.

The turning tools are of soft steel.*   They are purchased unshaped and the potter must learn to bend and
file them to suit himself.   A section of bench should be
set apart for filing and care must be taken that the steel
dust does not get into the clay.

One of the cylinders, with the bat upon which it was

* The Milligan Hardware Company, East Liverpool, Ohio.

thrown, is now taken in hand. Many beginners try to turn their pieces without detaching them from the bat, trusting to the original adhesion to hold the piece in position. This is a very unsatisfactory plan. A fundamental principle in craft work is that the mechanical difficulties in manipulation should be met and overcome at the beginning. If one trusts to some method which is apparently easy one walks with crutches and there will come a time, if progress is to be made, when such helps must of necessity be abandoned and then the learning must be begun again. Therefore the student is advised to face the mechanical technique at the very beginning. The cylinder may be turned on the throwing bat, but there is a better way.

The piece should not become so hard that it will release its hold on the bat but it should be cut away with a long-bladed knife. If the knife is held close to the bat a separation is easily effected. Set the leather-hard cylinder upon a new bat which is slightly damp and which runs true on the wheel. The first problem is to center the work. A pencil line may be run upon the bat making a circle just the size of the cylinder. Then as the wheel is revolved it will be seen if the piece runs true. It is quite unlikely that this will be the case. Perhaps the bottom is true but the top circle is untrue. In other words, the axis of the cylinder is not upright. Turn the cylinder upside down and see if it runs any better. If it does the work may be begun in this position. If it does not, turn it back again. Now take a pencil and hold it with a steady hand so that it just touches the near side as the wheel goes round. Lift up the edge of the cylinder on the side marked by the pencil and slip a morsel of clay

under it. Revolve the wheel and try with the pencil
again.   In this way raise or press down one side, keeping
the bottom circle in the center until both top and bottom
are running as nearly true as they can be made.   This,
so far, refers only to the horizontal planes.   If one side
is higher than the other it does not matter at present.
Now take three small pieces of soft clay, and, holding the
cylinder firmly with one hand, press them down at equi-
distant points in the angle where the piece joins the bat.
This serves to hold the work in position.   A square turning tool of small size is the best to begin with.   It is held
in the fingers as a pen is held but more firmly.   The
right hand rests on the turning stick and, the connection
between hand and stick being as rigid as possible, both
are moved together.   This is better at first than moving
the right hand freely, for this would surely result in irregular work.

The tool should be held so as to cut with one corner at
first and it is well to take one cut, remove the tool, take
another cut and so on.   The object should be to feel the
clay and to test its resistance.   No one can be a successful
potter who does not cultivate a sympathy for the clay.
The tool is to cut, not to scrape.   That is, the cutting
edge is to be opposed to the revolving clay.   The point
at which the tool touches the clay is opposite the center
or at the same distance from the operator as the center of
the wheel is.   If nearer to the workman the tool will not
cut; if farther away, it will scrape and pull (Fig. 5, page
34).

The first efforts should be directed toward acquiring
skill.   The student should endeavor to make a cut at any
desired point without regarding the effect upon the shape

of the cylinder. In other words, the clay is used merely as a practice piece. It is not to be preserved. It is a good plan to keep on turning the first piece until it is all turned away. Too many students fail because they wish to have a piece to keep. He will make the best ultimate success who cares nothing for the preservation of a dozen or two cylinders or other shapes, but uses them merely as exercises in manipulation. If the student is over anxious to avoid spoiling his work, he grows nervous and so loses control of his tools and material. To set no value on the practice pieces themselves begets confidence and this is the surest aid to success.

After two or three cylinders have been centered to the pencil line the attempt to center one free hand may be made. Place a cylinder on the wheel but not quite in the center. Spin the wheel at a medium rate. Fix the attention upon the eccentric motion, trying to forget the circular motion. As the cylinder appears to move from side to side tap it lightly with the hand so as to drive it toward the center. In all probability this will result in driving the cylinder off the wheel altogether. Some little practice is needed, but with perseverance the result will be a power of convenient and rapid centering which is never forgotten and which is the greatest possible aid to successful work. One may practice with a wooden cylinder or even a tin can if the weight approximates that of the clay pieces.

Accompanying the practice in turning there should be some exercise in the shaping and filing of tools. Broad tools filed to the proper curve are indispensable in finishing concave surfaces. A curved edge may also be put upon one or two narrow tools. These will cut more rapidly than the broader ones but will not leave as smooth a finish. Whatever tool is used the final surface must be worked over with a soft sponge and water so as to eliminate the tool marks and leave a plastic surface. One of the principal problems of the beginner is the vibration of the tool known as "chattering." This is sometimes so

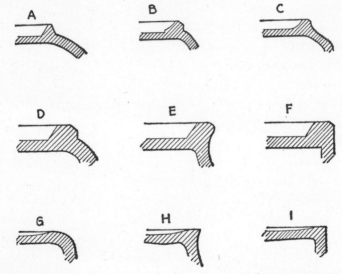

FIG. 20. Turned feet. *A B C*, feet for small pieces. *D E F*, feet for large pieces. *G H I*, common faults in foot finish.

slight as not to be felt by the hand but when the motion of the wheel is stopped the work will be found covered with fine ridges like gathering on muslin. This can be prevented by not using the broad edge of the tool until some experience has been gained. The ridges can be eliminated by going over the work again with a fine pointed tool and then using the sponge liberally. The point of the tool cuts through the small ribs or wrinkles whereas a broad tool would ride over them and make the trouble worse.

While the whole surface of the work will probably need more or less turning, the chief part of the operation is concerned with the under part or foot. The formation of a good foot marks a good potter and vice versa. Before beginning to turn it should be decided what kind of a foot is desired. Each shape has its own style. Some sketches are given here with an idea of the form to which each is adapted. They are shown upside down because the work is done in this position. The small bevel at the outer angle is used for facility in glazing. A foot finished thus always has a neat appearance when the glaze has been removed from the beveled face.

CHAPTER X

CUPS AND SAUCERS AND PLATES

IT is not likely that many craftsmen will care to produce table wares or even that they will be able to acquire the necessary skill. Simple as these wares seem, they are, in fact, the most difficult of all to make well. In factory working, one man makes nothing but cups, another saucers and another plates, so that each attains the skill of constant practice, but this is out of the question for the studio worker. At the same time it is well to know how it is done and it may be that some one will undertake to produce a few pieces for the sake of the enjoyment arising therefrom.

It is possible to finish a cup upon the wheel just as a vase is made. The handle is modeled in clay and fastened in place with slip when in the leather-hard condition. Saucers and plates cannot be made in this manner; first, because the broad thin bottom will surely crack and, second, because it is impracticable to turn a plate or saucer over in order to finish the bottom. The risk of breakage is so great that there is nothing to be gained.

If cups of uniform size are needed, they must be molded. The making of the molds has already been described. A small cylinder of the proper size is thrown in clay and removed from the wheel while soft. A number of these should be made at one time so as to avoid changing the wheel head often. When all are ready a hollow head shaped to receive the cup mold is set on the wheel and a mold inserted. One of the soft cylinders is now lowered gently into the mold and as the wheel is revolved the soft clay is pressed firmly against the walls with the fingers. A piece of wood, called a rib, cut to the exact shape of the inside of the cup, is used to smooth off the interior. The top edge is cut off and rounded and the mold is set aside for the cup to harden. As soon as the cup can be turned out it is set upside down upon the wheel and the bottom turned.

Another method dispenses with the formation of the cylinder or "lining." A ball of clay of the proper size is dropped into the mold and pressed into shape with the fingers, the wheel, of course, being spun. The finishing is accomplished with the rib as before. This method will answer for wares which are to receive a low fire but for high temperatures the clay must be handled by the first-named plan.

The cup is not complete without a handle. This may be modeled as already stated but to make each one of half a dozen in this way is unduly tedious. The better plan is to model a handle in wax and make a mold as already directed. A roll of soft clay is then laid in the mold, the two halves pressed together and the handle taken out and finished. Care must be taken that cup and handle are of the same degree of moisture, leather hard, for choice, or they will part company as they dry. The fastening is done with thick slip.

The method for saucers is the same as that for plates, so that one description will suffice. The first step is to make a tool or profile. A large handful of soft clay is rolled out into a thick cylinder and laid down upon the plate mold. It should extend from the center to the cir-cumference, forming a radius of the circle. The clay is pressed closely to the surface of the mold and part of it is squeezed into a knob which will form the hand-hold of the tool (Fig. 16, page 47). The clay is left in this position until it becomes nearly, but not quite, dry. It is then taken off and whittled into shape. The front edge must be straight and must lie along a radius of the plate. The foot is cut in at the proper point and a broad wedge-shaped hollow is made so as to gather the clay and pile it up into the foot. The hand-hold is shaped so as to fit comfortably between the first and second fingers of the right hand. When properly shaped the tool is thoroughly dried and then burned in the kiln. The fire must not be severe as it is important not to shrink the tool to any great extent. After burning slight corrections can be made with a file or a hard stone. The heel of the profile must be exactly at the center of the plate and the toe or curve must rest on the outer edge of the plate mold.

In making plates a "batting block" and "batter" are used. The former is a heavy block of plaster which is fixed to a strong table. It must be saturated with water when in use. The wedging table already described will serve for this. The batter is a disk of plaster to which a handle is attached. It may be made of a thick plaster block, the handle being cut out of the substance itself. This is also kept saturated with water so that the clay will not stick. A ball of clay is laid on the block and gently beaten out with the batter into a disk of the proper size and thickness. The face of this is then polished with a steel blade and the disk is lifted, turned over and laid, polished side downward, upon the mold. The wheel is then revolved and the clay pressed firmly to the mold with wet hands. The tool is dipped in water and pressed steadily upon the revolving clay. The heel must be adjusted accurately to the center and the foot will be seen to rise up in its proper place. The operation is not easy and many failures must be expected but practice will accomplish the desired result. When leather hard the plate is gone over with a thin piece of rubber and when quite hard it may be removed from the mold. The edge is trimmed and the face sponged over. The plate is then ready for the kiln.

CHAPTER XI

CASTING

IN commercial production the casting method is used constantly. It is a means of making light and delicate pieces with ease and, of course, all the pieces cast in the same mold are alike. This very fact, however, has led to the method being disregarded by the studio worker who does not wish to duplicate anything that he makes. If a single piece only is to be made the work involved in molding is a waste of time and it is better to strive for skill at the wheel, and yet there are occasions when a knowledge of casting is of great value. In the preparation of trial pieces there is no method better. To make these in sufficient number on the wheel would be tedious except for the benefit of the practice involved.

Directions for making molds have already been given and the slip which will have been prepared in the process of clay making is ready for the casting process. This slip should be thick, about the thickness of buckwheat batter. To be accurate, a pint should weigh 26 ounces. For small pieces or for vases with narrow necks it is advisable to use the slip rather thinner. For large wares, on the other hand, or for open bowls it may be slightly thicker. A few experiments will show the reason for this. Two quart jugs are needed. They should be large of neck and should deliver their contents freely and completely. Jugs with a deep shoulder are not good as the slips hangs in the pouring. One of these jugs is filled with slip which is to be poured carefully from one to the other, allowing it to flow gently down the side. This is to break the air bubbles which are nearly always present and the pouring should be repeated until the slip flows smooth and even.

The above method of preparing the casting slip will suffice for very simple forms. The working properties of the slip can be improved by the addition of one tenth to three tenths of 1 per cent of sodium silicate (water glass). This will allow the slip to become fluid with much less water, and thus decrease the shrinkage on drying.

The mold, being thoroughly dry, is tied around with twine, if in parts, and wedged firmly so that it cannot leak. The slip is then carefully poured so as not to touch the sides and the mold is filled until a small mound of slip rises over the edge. This mound will at once begin to sink as the water is drawn into the walls of the mold and slip must be added, little by little, to make good the loss. A small quantity of clay will now be found to have stiffened at the rim of the mold and if this be carefully removed with a steel tool the thickness of the wall of the vase will be seen. If not thick enough the mold must be continually filled up until the necessary thickness is attained. The mold is then carefully lifted, making sure that the bottom is held firmly, and the slip is poured out. It should not be poured back into the casting-jug but into another vessel.

The mold is now set upside down to drain. It should not be placed upon the table but upon two sticks laid parallel so that the drip may hang clear. Several molds may be filled in this way at one time and after about 20 minutes the one first filled may be opened. The bottom is gently detached and the upper part of the mold, consisting of two halves, is laid upon the table on its side. A little gentle manipulation will now suffice to lift the one half and the vase will be seen lying in the other half as in a cradle. The clay is still very soft and must be treated carefully. The half mold, with the contained vase, is taken in the left hand and held nearly upright, the fingers below, the thumb on the top. Now put the fingers of the right hand under the bottom of the vase, rest the thumb lightly against the side and tilt the half mold gently forward. If mold and clay are in good condition the vase will fall forward to be supported on the fingers of the right hand and steadied by the thumb. The half mold is now laid down and the vase taken in both hands, set gently on a plaster bat and put aside to dry. It often happens that the vase leaves the mold with reluctance. If the slip is very new, or the mold either damp or hard or worn out there will be some difficulty in effecting a separation. By allowing the work to stand a while, however, and by slightly jarring the mold from time to time with the ball of the thumb the piece can generally be removed without damage.

In using a new mold it is customary to make what is called a "waste filling." The mold is filled with slip and at once emptied. After standing a few minutes it is forcibly opened and the thin layer of clay inside is picked out with a ball of plastic clay pressed against it. A tool should never be used as this will damage the face of the mold. If the clay should stick obstinately a soft cloth used over the finger will remove it. The reason for this waste filling is that it removes the scum which occurs on all new molds.

Cast ware should not be touched until quite dry and then the spare at the neck is carefully cut off, the seams scraped down and the whole surface smoothed with fine sand paper and a soft cloth. Worn out linen serves excellently for this purpose.

Cups and bowls, if molded, are made without spare at the top. In this case great care must be taken to see that the edge is left clean and smooth in the casting. The spare neck on a vase acts as a margin of safety, as it is completely cut away in the finishing. If a piece has no spare the edge must be left without blemish at the first.

Chapter XII

GLAZES AND GLAZING

Introduction

MUCH of the fascination of pottery making is centered in the glaze; not only because of the beauty and usefulness it imparts to ware but also because of the challenge it presents to the craftsman. He who would be a potter soon realizes that he must learn about glazes and, once having so concluded, he becomes involved in a story as old and as intriguing as civilization itself.

At one time, a great deal of mystery surrounded the composition and production of glazes but the mystery has been dispelled. Present-day knowledge of glazes is very broad and, for a full understanding, a firm grasp of silicate chemistry is essential. However, a good deal may be learned by one not having a background in chemistry if one is willing to apply himself to the task. In the following treatment of the subject only such simple instruction as can be assimilated by one of ordinary intelligence will be attempted.

In his commendable desire to produce technically perfect glazes, the beginner often proceeds without sufficient thought to the records of previous workers. Such haste, though, perhaps leading to a knowledge of the mechanics of glazes, may leave much wanting as regards the appreciation of those values which determine their beauty and/or their appropriateness.

The student is urged to review the records of the past. He will find romance and inspiration in the story they unfold, and will be struck by the importance of the part played by glazes in the development of the art of pottery and the advancement of civilization. As the story unfolds, he will be impressed by the importance of each development and with the particular impetus each discovery gave to the art. He will gain an appreciation for the contributions made by the many workers of the past and for the obstacles they overcame. In the atmosphere of original discovery he will come to understand the subtleties of color and texture that contribute to the beauty of glazes and will vision the boundless field for future work.

Glazes can be defined as being impervious silicate coatings which are developed on ceramic articles by the fusion of mixtures of inorganic materials. These coatings serve several purposes: (1) they prevent the penetration of liquids; (2) they present a good-wearing, easily cleaned surface; and (3) they provide a vehicle for enriching the tactile and color properties of the form.

Glazes are prepared by mixing or milling fine silica (SiO_2) with other finely grained, inorganic materials. These mixtures are applied to ceramic ware and fired to a temperature which causes melting and fusion of the ingredients. Upon cooling, the melt solidifies, with or without crystallization and the glaze is formed.

Various earthy materials are used in compounding glazes. These materials may be the source of one, two, three or even more oxides. It is in the light of the oxide (or oxides) which a material supplies that the ceramist considers it. Before one can intelligently use a material, he must know its chemical composition and the effects of its oxide content on the behavior and properties of the resulting glaze. Therefore, preliminary to the listing of ingredients, consideration will be given to the principal oxides making up glazes and the primary functions of these oxides.

In general, oxides contain:

A. One atom of element and one atom of oxygen.
Examples: Certain metallic oxides—lead oxide (PbO), zinc oxide (ZnO); the alkaline earth oxides—calcium oxide (CaO), barium oxide (BaO), magnesium oxide (MgO).

B. Two atoms of element and one atom of oxygen.
Examples: the alkalies; potassium oxide (K_2O) and sodium oxide (Na_2O).

C. Two atoms of element and three atoms of oxygen.
Examples: aluminum oxide (Al_2O_3), boron oxide (B_2O_3).

D. One atom of element and two atoms of oxygen.
Examples: silicon oxide (SiO_2), titanium oxide (TiO_2), tin oxide (SnO_2) and zirconium oxide (ZrO_2).

The ceramist classifies the oxides according to their acidity and in writing a glaze formula he places like oxides together. For convenience these are arranged in a structure or formula having three groupings called: (A) RO or R_2O, (B) R_2O_3 and (C) RO_2. The oxides of group (A) and group (B) are basic and the ceramist places them in the RO or R_2O column of his formula. The oxides of group (C) are neutral oxides and are placed in the R_2O_3 column of the formula and the oxides of group (D) which are acid are placed in the RO_2 column. The place occupied by the various oxides in a glaze formula are as follows:

RO or R_2O	R_2O_3	RO_2
PbO		
ZnO		SiO_2
K_2O	Al_2O_3	TiO_2
Na_2O	B_2O_3	SnO_2
CaO		ZrO_2
BaO		
MgO		

BUILDING A GLAZE

From the great number of materials that can be incorporated into glazes, a selection of the more important ones has been made. These materials are listed in the following table (page 88). From these materials, it is possible to produce all types of glazes.

One of the most simple glazes (temperature 750–800° C) is a lead silicate having the glaze formula:

$$PbO\dots\dots\dots 1.0\} \quad \{SiO_2\dots\dots\dots 1.0$$

This formula indicates that the glaze is made by mixing 1 mol of PbO (lead oxide) with 1 mol of SiO_2 (silica). A mol is a mass equivalent numerically to the molecular weight of a substance. It is usually expressed as grams but can also be expressed in pounds or ounces. In glaze calculations, one system should be selected and adhered to. By reference to the table in which molecular weights are given, it is found that the molecular weight of PbO is 223 and that of SiO_2 is 60. Therefore, by mixing 223 parts by weight of PbO with 60 parts by weight of SiO_2 the glaze can be prepared.

PbO can be supplied by litharge, the formula of which is PbO and the SiO_2 can be supplied by flint, the formula

Commercial Name	Chemical Name	Symbol or Formula	Molecular Weight
1. Barium Carbonate	Barium Carbonate	$BaCO_3$	197
2. Borax*	Sodium Tetra-Borate	$Na_2O\text{-}2B_2O_3\text{-}10H_2O$	382
3. Boric Acid	Boric Acid	$B_2O_3\text{-}3H_2O$	124
4. Colemanite	Calcium Borate	$2CaO\text{-}3B_2O_3\text{-}5H_2O$	412
5. Dolomite	Calcium-Magnesium Carbonate	$CaCO_3\text{-}MgCO_3$	184
6. Feldspar (Soda)†	Albite	$Na_2O\text{-}Al_2O_3\text{-}6SiO_2$	524
7. Feldspar (Potash)†	Orthoclase	$K_2O\text{-}Al_2O_3\text{-}6iSO_2$	556
8. Flint	Silica	SiO_2	60
9. Kaolin or China Clay	Aluminum Silicate	$Al_2O_3\text{-}2SiO_2\text{-}2H_2O$	258
10. Magnesite	Magnesium Carbonate	$MgCO_3$	84
11. Niter*	Potassium Nitrate	KNO_3	101
12. Soda Ash*	Sodium Carbonate	Na_2CO_3	106
13. Talc	Magnesium Silicate	$3MgO\text{-}4SiO_2\text{-}H_2O$	378
14. Tin Oxide	Tin Oxide	SnO_2	151
15. Titanium Oxide	Titanium Oxide	TiO_2	80
16. White Lead	Lead Carbonate	$2PbCO_3\text{-}Pb(OH)_2$	775
17. Whiting	Calcium Carbonate	$CaCO_3$	100
18. Zinc Oxide	Zinc Oxide	ZnO	81
19. Zirconium Oxide	Zirconium Oxide	ZrO_2	123
20. Zirconium Silicate	Zirconium Silicate	$ZrO_2\text{-}SiO_2$	183

* Soluble in water. See notes under fritted glazes.

† The compositions of commercial feldspars vary considerably. Not only do all potash feldspars contain some soda and all soda feldspars contain some potash but also the Al_2O_3 and SiO_2 contents will vary. The formulas given are for ideal feldspars, but may be used if the actual composition of the feldspar being used is unknown.

of which is SiO_2. Therefore a batch of this glaze would be:

Litharge...................... 223 parts by weight
Flint.......................... 60 parts by weight

Litharge is not, however, a very satisfactory material to use as a source of lead oxide for a glaze. It is very heavy (per unit volume) and does not mix well with water. The material most generally used for the introduction of PbO is white lead, the molecular formula of which is $2PbCO_3 \cdot Pb(OH)_2$.

This formula when broken down is as follows:

$$2PbCO_3 = 2PbO \cdot 2CO_2$$
$$Pb(OH)_2 = PbO \cdot H_2O$$

$$2PbCO_3 \cdot Pb(OH)_2 = 3PbO \cdot 2CO_2 \cdot H_2O$$

1 mol of white lead = 3 mols of lead oxide + 2 mols of carbon dioxide*
                                                 + 1 mol of water

In using white lead to furnish the lead oxide for the glaze under consideration, it would be necessary to divide the molecular weight of white lead by 3 because 1 mol of PbO is indicated in the formula. Inasmuch as the molecular weight of white lead is 775, one third of this, or 258.3 parts by weight, would furnish 1 mol of PbO, the same amount of lead oxide furnished by 223 parts by weight of litharge. The mixture for practical purposes would be:

White Lead................... 258 parts by weight
Flint........................ 60 parts by weight

. which, when mixed, ground, spread and fired on the ware would produce a very fusible glaze of a yellowish tone.

. Although this simple silicate of lead would be a glaze under certain conditions, it is found to possess three faults:

* CO_2 or H_2O contained in the material goes off during firing and hence do not become part of the fired glaze.

1. It is too fluid under fire. The glaze will flow down inclined and vertical surfaces and leave the upper edges of the piece bare.

2. If subjected to a long, slow fire, it will devitrify,† thereby resulting in a finish of little gloss.

3. This glaze scratches easily.

These faults may be corrected by the addition of Al_2O_3 (aluminum oxide) to the glaze. This oxide is most generally and most satisfactorily introduced by the addition of clay (China clay or kaolin), the formula of which is $Al_2O_3 \cdot 2SiO_2 \cdot 2H_2O$. (Clay is not only a very satisfactory source of Al_2O_3 but its presence in a glaze facilitates preparation and application of the glaze.) Attention is called to the fact that clay supplies 2 mols of SiO_2 with each mol of Al_2O_3. (The water ($2H_2O$) as in the case of white lead is lost during the firing.)

It has been found that the incorporation of .2 mols of aluminum oxide is generally sufficient in a low-temperature glaze. However, the addition of this amount of Al_2O_3 to the glaze under discussion would not only cure its faults but would result in a finish of low brilliance. Because of this, it has been found necessary to increase the SiO_2 content along with the increase in Al_2O_3. (Because SiO_2 is the principal glass-forming oxide, it must be present in sufficient quantity to satisfy all the other oxides if a satisfactory glaze is to be obtained.) In low-temperature glazes, such as the one under discussion, it has been found that there should be 1 mol of silica for

† Devitrification appears as a dull scum, sometimes in patches and around the edges of the ware. It is, in fact (in this case), a crystallization of silica which separates out as a salt does from an evaporating brine.

each mol of RO ingredients, and in addition 3 mols of SiO_2 for each mol of Al_2O_3.

The glaze formula then becomes:

$$PbO \ldots \ldots 1.0\} \quad Al_2O_3 \ldots \ldots .2 \quad \{SiO_2 \ldots \ldots 1.6$$

Because this formula is more complicated than those discussed heretofore, it would be well to recalculate the entire batch pointing out the fundamental steps to be followed in all "formula to batch" calculations.

First the items in the formula are extended in a horizontal line, space being left on one side for the list of ingredients.

Material	Mols		PbO	Al_2O_3	SiO_2
White Lead	$\dfrac{1.0}{3}$	Mols to be supplied	1.0	.2	1.6
		Supplies	1.0		
Clay	.2	To be supplied	0	.2	1.6
		Supplies		.2	.4
Flint	1.2	To be supplied		0	1.2
		Supplies			1.2
		To be supplied			0

Each item is thus disposed of until the list is complete. It should be noted that 1 mol of white lead contains 3 mols of PbO; therefore, it is necessary to use only 1/3 mol of the material for 1 mol of PbO.

The figures are given in mols and each must be multiplied by the molecular weight of the material used.

Material	Mols	Molecular Weight	Parts by Weight
White Lead......	$\frac{1.0}{3}$ (1/3)	775	258.3
Clay...........	.2	258	51.6
Flint...........	1.2	60	72.0

This is a glaze of the same character as that first given except that it neither flows unduly down the inclined surfaces of the ware nor devitrifies in a long-continued fire. However, because of the alumina and increased silica, the maturing temperature of the glaze has been increased approximately 100° C.

A glaze with only lead oxide as the base (in the RO group) is not desirable for general use. The color is yellowish and the lead oxide is apt to destroy the hue of any colors which are used with it. Therefore, the introduction of another base is in order. For the sake of example and to permit the use of a material supplying three oxides, potassium oxide (K_2O) will be introduced. The formula will be written:

$$\left.\begin{array}{l} PbO\ldots\ldots\, .9 \\ K_2O\ldots\ldots\, .1 \end{array}\right\} Al_2O_3\ldots\ldots\, .2 \ \{SiO_2\ldots\ldots\, 1.6$$

The sum of the mols in the RO group is always brought to unity. The reason for this is that if one formula is to be compared with another, there must be a uniform basis upon which to work, and furthermore, it makes no difference whether the silica combines with one, two, three or four bases, the chemical action is similar and, so long as the sum of the bases is kept at unity, the same amount of silica will be required.

The batch will be determined as before, using potash feldspar as a source of K_2O.

Material	Mols		PbO	K_2O	Al_2O_3	SiO_2
White Lead	$\dfrac{1.0}{3} \times .9$	Mols to be supplied	.9	.1	.2	1.6
		Supplies	.9			
Potash Feldspar	.1	To be supplied	0	.1	.2	1.6
		Supplies		.1	.1	.6
Clay	.1	To be supplied		0	.1	1.0
		Supplies			.1	.2
Flint	.8	To be supplied			0	.8
		Supplies				.8
		To be supplied				0

Then to determine the actual weights to use:

Material	Mols	Molecular Weight	Parts by Weight
White Lead........	.3	775	232.5
Potash Feldspar....	.1	556	55.6
Clay.............	.1	258	25.8
Flint.............	.8	60	48.0
		Total	361.9

In this manner glazes can be built and compared with one another intelligently. Simple experiments using other oxides should be tried to determine their effects on the glaze and on the colors used with it. In selecting the RO ingredients with which to build a glaze it is desirable to use one at least from each group but it must be borne in mind that however many bases we introduce the total must always be unity. For example, the following groups are set forth:

1. PbO Lead Oxide.............. .7
   Calcium Oxide........... .3
   —————
   RO....... 1.0

2. PbO........ .6
   CaO........ .4
   —————
   RO..... 1.0

3. PbO Lead Oxide.............. .5
   ZnO Zinc Oxide.............. .2
   CaO Calcium Oxide........... .3
   —————
   RO....... 1.0

4. PbO........ .6
   ZnO.. 1
   CaO........ .3
   —————
   RO..... 1.0

5. PbO Lead Oxide.............. .6
   CaO Calcium Oxide........... .3
   K_2O Potassium Oxide.......... .1
   —————
   RO....... 1.0

6. PbO........ .50
   CaO........ .35
   K_2O........ .15
   —————
   RO..... 1.00

7. PbO Lead Oxide.............. .45
   ZnO Zinc Oxide.............. .10
   CaO Calcium Oxide........... .30
   K_2O Potassium Oxide.......... .15
   —————
   RO....... 1.00

8. PbO........ .35
   ZnO........ .15
   CaO........ .35
   K_2O........ .15
   —————
   RO..... 1.00

The glazes, so far discussed, have been what are termed raw, bright, transparent, colorless glazes. They are called raw glazes because the materials used in compounding them are naturally occurring minerals or compounds commercially available, all of which are insoluble in water. They are called bright glazes because of the high reflectivity of their surfaces. They are called transparent glazes because one can see through them to the body upon which they are fired. They are called colorless glazes because no material has been added that would produce a color.

Fritted Glazes. It is frequently desirable to use a water-soluble material such as borax ($Na_2O \cdot 2B_2O_3 \cdot 10H_2O$). Ordinary glaze preparation methods do not permit the use of such materials; consequently special steps have to be taken in order to use them. The water-soluble material is mixed with other selected glaze materials and melted to form a glass. This glass is known as a frit and has a definite composition. It is water-chilled, ground and then incorporated into the glaze proper. Glazes made containing frits are called fritted glazes.

The following is an example of a fritted glaze:

$$\left.\begin{array}{ll} PbO \ldots \ldots & .30 \\ ZnO \ldots \ldots & .15 \\ CaO \ldots \ldots & .25 \\ Na_2O \ldots \ldots & .20 \\ K_2O \ldots \ldots & .10 \end{array}\right\} \quad \left.\begin{array}{ll} Al_2O_3 \ldots \ldots & .15 \\ B_2O_3 \ldots \ldots & .40 \end{array}\right\} \quad SiO_2 \ldots \ldots 2.65$$

This will be produced in accordance with the usual calculation by the mix.

Parts by Weight

White Lead	$\frac{.3}{3} \times 775 =$	77.5
Zinc Oxide	$.15 \times 81 =$	12.1
Whiting	$.25 \times 100 =$	25.0 (all to go into frit)
Borax	$.20 \times 382 =$	76.4 (all to go into frit)
Potash Feldspar	$.10 \times 556 =$	55.6 (30 parts to go into frit)
Kaolin	$.05 \times 258 =$	12.9
Flint	$1.95 \times 60 =$	117.0 (50 parts to go into frit)

The borax contains the required amount of soda and boric oxide and the potash is supplied by the feldspar. Borax, being soluble, must be melted with certain other ingredients into an insoluble glass. Thus,

Frit:

Parts by Weight

Borax	$76.4 \times 2 =$	152.8
Whiting	$25 \times 2 =$	50.0
Feldspar	$30 \times 2 =$	60.0
Flint	$50 \times 2 =$	100.0
		362.8

These ingredients are weighed out in double quantity to guard against loss in melting and are fused either in the kiln or in a special furnace. When using a special furnace, the charge is put into a refractory crucible and, when melted, is poured out into water. This breaks up the frit and renders it easy to grind. A similar crucible may be used in the kiln but, as the frit becomes very hard when cold, and is difficult to grind, the special furnace method is better. If the frit, as given, proves too sluggish to pour freely, the feldspar may be omitted, being added, of course, to the glaze mix. The melted weight of the frit must now be calculated.

In each mol of borax, there are 180 parts of water. Whiting contains 44 parts of carbon dioxide. Both water and carbon dioxide pass off during the melting, thus the 76.4 parts of borax will be reduced to 40.5 parts, and the 25 parts of whiting will be reduced to 14 parts. The feldspar and flint lose nothing. Therefore, the frit after melting will be:

	Parts by Weight
Borax	40.5
Whiting	14.0
Feldspar	30.0
Flint	50.0
	134.5

and the final mix for the glaze will be:

	Parts by Weight
Frit	134.5
White Lead	77.5
Zinc Oxide	12.1
Feldspar	25.6
Kaolin	12.9
Flint	67.0

Fritted glazes are better than raw glazes for certain classes of ware. They are usually whiter and less easily scratched. They are, moreover, better for use with underglaze colors and are, as a rule, more easily melted. It is never necessary to make a frit for the preparation of matt glazes.

/ *Matt Glazes.* The texture of the matt glaze is always pleasing and the artist is not content unless at least some of his work can be finished in this way.

Matt glazes are not underfired glazes nor are they produced by the treatment of a glaze by acid or sand blast. It was mentioned earlier that a glaze free from alumina will devitrify or become dull. This is undesirable when a glaze is intended to be brilliant but it may be controlled and turned to advantage in the production of a certain type of matt. The successful preparation of this silica matt is extremely difficult. In fact, in the studio kiln it is almost impossible. These small kilns are apt to cool with great rapidity whereas, in order to produce the silica matt, the kiln must be cooled very slowly, *hours and even days* of cooling being sometimes necessary.

The alumina matt is more simple and its texture is quite satisfactory, being, in the opinion of some, the more pleasing of the two. The RO content of this type of glaze may consist of any of the bases used in bright glazes, the proportion of each being adjusted in accordance with the desired point of fusion. The alumina content is rather higher than in a bright glaze and should not fall much below .3 mol, .35 mol is even better. The silica content in matt glazes is very often limited to the amount furnished by the feldspar and clay, as is the case in the following glaze. The texture of the glaze may be altered by increasing the silica content slightly.

In the RO group, lead oxide is desirable up to .5 and it is advantageous to introduce K_2O (with feldspar). Calcium oxide is also good and zinc oxide can be used sparingly. The high alumina content necessitates a good deal of clay and as this, if used raw, would make the glaze too plastic and cause it to crack, it is best to calcine a part of it, thus removing the combined water and changing the weight from 258 to 222. The calculation will then proceed as in the case of a bright glaze.

$$PbO \ldots \ldots .50$$
$$CaO \ldots \ldots .35 \qquad Al_2O_3 \ldots \ldots .35 \qquad SiO_2 \ldots \ldots 1.30$$
$$K_2O \ldots \ldots .15$$

$$RO \ldots 1.00$$

			PbO	CaO	K_2O	Al_2O_3	SiO_2
White Lead	$\frac{1.0}{3} \times .5$	To be supplied	.50	.35	.15	.35	1.30
		Supplies	.50				
Whiting	.35	To be supplied	0	.35	.15	.35	1.30
		Supplies		.35			
Feldspar	.15	To be supplied		0	.15	.35	1.30
		Supplies			.15	.15	.90
Calcined Kaolin	.15	To be supplied			0	.20	.40
		Supplies				.15	.30
Kaolin (Raw)	.05	To be supplied				.05	.10
		Supplies				.05	.10
		To be supplied					0

The mix therefore is:

Parts by Weight

White Lead	$\frac{.50}{3} \times 775 =$	129.2
Whiting	$.35 \times 100 =$	35.0
Potash Feldspar	$.15 \times 556 =$	83.4
Calcined Kaolin	$.15 \times 222 =$	33.3
Kaolin	$.05 \times 258 =$	12.9

Total   293.8

This will give a silky matt glaze, nearly white, maturing at about cone 1. If a lower fusing point is desired the white lead may be increased at the expense of the whiting or, if the glaze proves too fusible, the reverse will correct it. Attention is called to the fact that the preparation and application of matt glazes are of particular importance (see glaze preparation and application).

Colored Glazes. The range of colors obtainable in glazes will depend upon glaze composition, temperature of firing, condition of firing and coloring oxides used. Each ceramist should develop his own palette of color by experimentation. The principal coloring oxides are shown in the following table. The molecular weights of the oxides are given but it should be noted that, in general, the addition of a coloring oxide is made by adding a desired number of parts by weight to a weighed batch of glaze.

Color	Chemical Name	Symbol or Formula	Molecular Weight
Blue	Black Cobalt Oxide	Co_3O_4	241
	Cobalt Carbonate	$CoCO_3$	119
Blue and Green	Copper Oxide	CuO	80
	Copper Carbonate	$CuCO_3 \cdot Cu(OH)_2$	221
Brown	Manganese Dioxide	MnO_2	87
	Manganese Carbonate	$MnCO_3$	115
Red-brown and Amber-yellow	Iron Oxide (Ferric)	Fe_2O_3	160
Brown and Grey	Ferric Chromate	$Fe_2(CrO_4)_3 \cdot - 2Fe_2O_3$	780
Green, Grey and Brown	Chromium Oxide	Cr_2O_3	152
	Nickel Oxide	NiO	75
Yellow	Uranium Oxide	U_2O_5	556
	Sodium Uranate	$Na_2U_2O_7$	634

Naples yellow (red lead, antimony, tin) and vanadium stains are used for most yellows at the present time because uranium is not available.

Pinks to red to maroon colors are produced from chrome, tin, and calcium stains.

The number of colors and color effects are limitless. For most glazes the following coloring oxides and oxide combinations will produce the colors mentioned (additions to be made to approximately 300 grams of glaze).

Blue

Grams

Cobalt Oxide............ 3

Slate Blue

Cobalt Oxide............ 3
Nickel Oxide............ 1

Warm Blue

Cobalt Oxide............ 2
Iron Oxide.............. 1

Green

Copper Oxide........... 8

Blue Green

Grams

Copper Oxide........... 8
Cobalt Oxide............ 1

Cool Green

Copper Oxide........... 8
Cobalt Oxide............ 1
Nickel Oxide............ 2

Olive Green

Copper Oxide........... 6
Iron Oxide.............. 4

Orange Brown

Iron Oxide.............. 8

	Grams		*Grams*
Red Brown		Yellow	
Iron Oxide	8	Yellow Stain	8
Chrome Oxide	1	Uranium Oxide	3
Zinc Oxide	3		

It will be appreciated that varying tones can be had by increasing or decreasing the amounts indicated.

Attention is called to the notes on colored glazes in the section on glaze preparation.

Opaque Glazes. Opaque glazes can be obtained by adding SnO_2 or ZrO_2 to a glaze. An opaque so-called "tin enamel" (cone 02) is as follows:

Formula

$$\left.\begin{array}{l} PbO \dots \dots .40 \\ CaO \dots \dots .25 \\ K_2O \dots \dots .20 \\ ZnO \dots \dots .15 \end{array}\right\} \quad Al_2O_3 \dots \dots .25 \quad \left\{\begin{array}{l} SiO_2 \dots \dots .75 \\ SnO_2 \dots \dots .20 \end{array}\right.$$

Batch

White Lead	103.2
Whiting	25.0
Feldspar	111.0
Zinc Oxide	12.1
Kaolin	12.9
Flint	27.0
Tin Oxide	30.2
Total	321.4

Zirconium oxide (ZrO_2) may be used as an opacifier in place of tin oxide but it is necessary to use about 50 per cent more to produce the desired opacity. Zirconium silicate is commonly used as a source of ZrO_2 in glazes.

Alkaline Glazes. Glazes that have a high soda and potash content are called alkaline glazes. The brilliant glazes that can be produced with this type of glaze are intriguing to the ceramist. Alkaline glazes are very difficult to prepare from a raw batch and special consideration has to be given to the bodies upon which they are applied. The high alkali content results in glazes having high thermal expansion which accounts for their tendency to craze.

The formula of a typical alkaline glaze is given herewith:

Na$_2$O....... .60
K$_2$O........ .10   Al$_2$O$_3$....... .10   SiO$_2$....... 1.30
CaO........ .30

For color, add the following to the batch:

Egyptian Blue, Opaque.........Black Oxide of Copper (2 to 4 per cent)
                              Tin Oxide (7 per cent)
Persian Blue, Opaque...........Black Oxide of Copper (3 to 5 per cent)
                              Tin Oxide (7 per cent)
Sapphire Blue.................Black Oxide of Cobalt (.5 per cent)
Aubergine....................Manganese Dioxide (4 per cent)

In a glaze of this type, all ingredients, excepting the clay, should be fritted.

Frits of this type can be purchased from one of the companies listed in the back of the book and will give more dependable results than can be obtained with water-soluble raw alkaline glazes.

PREPARATION AND APPLICATION

Preparation. The first step in preparing a glaze is weighing out the ingredients. For this purpose, a beam balance which eliminates loose weights is most practical. The balance should be equipped with a suitable scoop in which to place the materials. It will be found convenient to use metric weights, thus eliminating much of the calculation involved in the use of pounds and ounces. The capacity of the balance should be 1 kilogram (1000 grams). One beam of the balance should be graduated in 0.1 gram intervals.

After the glaze is weighed, it must be very thoroughly

mixed. The mixing is usually done wet. Sufficient water is added to bring the batch to the consistency of heavy cream (between 50 and 70 per cent of the weight of dry ingredients). The mixing can be done by hand in a porcelain mortar but a better mixing will be obtained if accomplished in a pebble mill. A pebble mill consists of a porcelain jar which is set in a frame and made to revolve upon its axis in a horizontal position (60 rpm). The mill is about half filled with porcelain or flint pebbles which perform the mixing as they roll against each other. Considerably more grinding is accomplished in the pebble mill than in the porcelain mortar and in some glazes where coarse materials are present, this is highly desirable. A mill of 1 gallon capacity is most commonly used and is most generally satisfactory. After approximately 1 hour of milling, the jar is taken from the frame and the glaze removed. The jar and pebbles are washed with an excess of water and the washings saved. The glaze is then strained through a sieve (100 to 120 mesh), set aside to settle and the clear water siphoned off.

It is frequently desired to condition a glaze, or to improve its working consistency for the type of application to be employed. This is accomplished by the addition of effective materials to the glaze either before or after milling. Gum tragacanth, gum arabic, sodium alginate, magnesium sulphate, calcium nitrate, calcium chloride and certain commercial conditioners are used for this purpose. The amount used is very small. In the case of gums, it is usual to add a tablespoonful of the prepared gum to a batch of 300 grams of glaze. If dry salts are used about 1 per cent of the dry batch by weight is added.

Application. When a glaze is to be applied by dipping, the specific gravity of the glaze (weight of glaze per unit volume as compared to water) will vary depending upon the porosity of the ware to be glazed. For average ware the specific gravity will vary from 1.5 to 1.7. When very porous ware is to be glazed, it is desirable to saturate it before dipping. This prevents the accumulation of too heavy a coat and the necessity of using a glaze of very low specific gravity.

The thickness of the application will vary greatly depending upon the type of glaze and the effect desired. For ordinary work, the glaze is applied to a thickness of .025 inch. Matt glazes and textural glazes are applied heavier, frequently as much as two or three times the normal thickness.

Spraying is also used as a method of applying a glaze. The porosity of the ware is not as important as in the case of dipping because the thickness of the coat can be more readily controlled. A very dry spray application is not recommended because the glaze is easily disturbed or rubbed off during handling. If it is desired to use a comparatively dry spray, the disadvantages may be overcome by finishing off with a slightly wet application. This will consolidate the glaze and produce a smooth finish. Gums, used in conditioning the glaze, also improve the handling properties by adding dry strength to the glaze.

The word "engobe," when used as a ceramic term, refers to a thin coating of clay, also called a slip, laid over a coarse body to give a different color or texture. For routine work prepared engobes may be bought from supply houses, but for original work the potter had best experiment with his own mixtures.

Engobes are usually composed of china clay, flint and feldspar much as a white earthenware body is constituted but with a larger content of flint. The clay content in such a mixture should be regulated with a due regard for shrinkage. For example, an engobe which is to be applied over a dry clay or over a bisk body should have a lower content of clay than one intended for application on damp or leather hard ware. Slips prepared for use at low temperatures sometimes contain small percentages of fluxing material, in the form of frit or ground glass, to insure greater density. As in the case of glazes a wide variety of color additions is possible.

Engobes may be applied in a variety of ways. Special effects can be had by dipping or sponging, and by the use of brushes, quills and stencils.

Typical Glazes

While the purpose of this work is not so much to put ready-made materials into the hands of the craftsman as to enable him to work out his own plans, it is recognized that there are some workers who lack the training and even the patience to do this. For these, the following glazes are given, but with the proviso that no formula can be regarded as perfect for all conditions. Just as an untrained cook can spoil a dinner even when surrounded by cookery books, so the best of formulas will fail when unskillfully treated. One must be prepared to recognize the faults which are sure to develop and to correct them in an intelligent manner. The previous chapters should therefore be carefully studied, not alone for the information but because "the joy of working" depends greatly upon the knowledge one has of the operations involved and a modest confidence in one's own powers.

1. Bright raw glaze.

Cone .06   *Formula*

$$\left.\begin{array}{l} PbO \dots \dots .65 \\ CaO \dots \dots .25 \\ K_2O \dots \dots .10 \end{array}\right\} \quad Al_2O_3 \dots \dots .15 \quad SiO_2 \dots \dots 1.45$$

Mix:

White Lead	168
Whiting	25
Feldspar	56
Kaolin	13
Flint	45

Grind, with one-half pint of water, for 1 hour.

2. Bright raw glaze.

Cone 1   *Formula*

$$\left.\begin{array}{l} PbO \dots \dots .45 \\ ZnO \dots \dots .15 \\ CaO \dots \dots .25 \\ K_2O \dots \dots .15 \end{array}\right\} \quad Al_2O_3 \dots \dots .20 \quad SiO_2 \dots \dots 1.60$$

Mix:

White Lead	116
Whiting	25
Zinc Oxide	12
Feldspar	83
Kaolin	13
Flint	36

3. Bright fritted glaze.

Cone .02   *Formula*

$$\left.\begin{array}{l} PbO \dots \dots .25 \\ ZnO \dots \dots .15 \\ CaO \dots \dots .30 \\ Na_2O \dots \dots .20 \\ K_2O \dots \dots .10 \end{array}\right\} \quad \left.\begin{array}{l} Al_2O_3 \dots \dots .15 \\ B_2O_3 \dots \dots .30 \end{array}\right\} \quad SiO_2 \dots \dots 2.35$$

Mix:

Frit		Glaze	
Borax	114	Frit	117
Whiting	60	White Lead	64
Soda Ash	10	Zinc Oxide	12
Spar	56	Spar	28
Flint	78	Kaolin	13
		Flint	60

Grind as before.

4. Matt glaze.

Cone .02   *Formula*

PbO .... .50

CaO .... .30 Al_2O_3 .... .34 SiO_2 .... 1.48

K_2O .... .20

Mix:

White Lead	129
Whiting	30
Spar	111
Calcined Kaolin	22
Kaolin	11

5. Matt glaze.

Cone 7   *Formula*

CaO .... .75
K_2O .... .25 $\Big\}$ Al_2O_3 .... .55 SiO_2 .... 2.10

Mix:

Feldspar	139
Whiting	75
Calcined Kaolin	55
Kaolin	13

THE DEFECTS OF GLAZES

While it may chance that body and glaze and fire are so adjusted that faults do not develop, this state of things is rare. Besides, it is always possible that an occasional trouble may arise, hence it will be well to recount a few of the commonest defects with the method of cure. A cure is not necessarily specific. There may be a complication of causes but the remedy indicates the line along which relief will be found.

1. Crazing. Fine cracks appear in the glaze but do not penetrate the body. There are many causes. The body may be underfired or overfired. In the former case the crazing does not always appear at once and it grows worse upon standing. In the latter case the glaze is found to be crazed when taken from the kiln and it does not extend even after long standing. The glaze may be underfired. In this case the lines of the crack are broken and irregular, one often changing its direction without meeting another crack. In all these cases the remedy is obvious.

Crazing also occurs when both body and glaze are correctly fired but when there is an inherent disagreement in expansion. In such a case a little flint added either to the body or to the glaze will tend to cure the trouble but it must be remembered that the addition of flint to the glaze is apt to render it less fusible and therefore, while one craze may be cured, another may be caused. The addition of flint to the body is the simplest remedy.

2. Shivering or peeling. This is the reverse of crazing and is caused by the glaze being too large for the body. It almost always appears immediately upon cooling the ware. The edges or convex surfaces push off and even the ware itself is shattered. The remedy is to decrease the flint in either body or glaze.

3. Blistering. Glazes, both bright and matt, are apt to develop blisters at times. These may be yet unbroken when the kiln is opened or they may have melted down to a small crater, a ring with a depression in the center. The cause of this fault is usually to be found in the body.

Many clays contain sulphur which tends to produce a scum on the ware. This is more pronounced in clays that have been aged. The glaze attacks this sulphate scum and a gas is generated which boils out and causes blisters. If old clay blisters and new clay does not it may be regarded as certain that this is the cause. A little barium carbonate added to the clay will help to effect a cure. About 1 per cent is usually enough. If the cause be not found in the clay it may exist in the glaze itself. Some glaze ingredients contain impurities in the form of sulphates and these will cause blisters.

4. The glaze flows, leaving bare places. It is too fluid, add a little clay and flint.

5. A matt glaze burns to a bright surface. Matt glazes must be used in a very thick coat. If too thin they will inevitably brighten. The fire may be too high. The fire may be "reducing," that is, with insufficient air.

6. The glaze crawls or rolls up in lumps. Notice whether the glaze is cracked before burning. If so it will surely crawl. Too fine grinding is usually the cause of this trouble. Too much clay in the glaze may cause it, or a too porous body. A body which is underfired will almost certainly cause the glaze to crawl.

7. Pinholes appear in the glaze when cool. Too rapid cooling is the cause.

CHAPTER XIII

THE FIRE

KILNS and burning form the pivot upon which the art of the potter turns. Let it be at once understood that he who finds it impossible to procure and manage a kiln had best take to some other craft.

Kilns are of two types, "open-fire" and "muffle." In the open-fire kiln the flames pass through the firing chamber and the ware may be exposed to their action, as in stoneware and brick; or it may be enclosed in the fire clay cases, called "saggers," as in many forms of pottery, dishes, or faience. The muffle kiln is a closed chamber which is surrounded by flames but which is not entered by them. This, or other form of protection from direct contact with the flames and combustion gases, is necessary in the production and control of most ceramic colors and decorations. Portable studio kilns and others used by small-scale producers employ varied adaptations of the muffle principle of construction.

Kilns are further described as to:

1. The fuel used.
2. The method of introducing the fuel, and of removing the products of combustion.
3. Type of ware to be produced and the temperature range required.

The solid fuels, wood or coal, can be used in firing ceramic ware. Although these fuels have definite advantages in the production of special wares, they are impractical for the average individual potter. Except in rural areas which have a supply of low-cost or part-time labor, accessible sources of fuel, and freedom from zoning restrictions, the cost and trouble of firing with wood or coal will outweigh any advantages that may be gained.

Natural gas is the most efficient fuel but it is not always available. Manufactured or "city gas" is more costly, but adequate, if feed lines and burners make the necessary provision for the lower heat potential.

Vaporized oil is an excellent and economical fuel. Special pumps and electric blowers are necessary but the added cost of these items may be balanced against lower cost per firing. Kerosene may be burned by direct gravity flow and without special blowers. Such kilns require careful and constant supervision and must be connected to a chimney having an especially good draft.

The selection of a suitable kiln is determined by local conditions, financial considerations, and by the kind and amount of ware to be produced. The question is often asked: "Can I build my own kiln?" Possibly so, but probably not a very good one. Reliable kiln construction requires specialized training, skill and experience. The beginner who does not wish to risk the loss of time and construction materials, and endure the frustrations caused by an undependable tool is advised to consult a professional kiln engineer or manufacturer. Even when suitable plans are available, the construction should be supervised by an experienced ceramist.

Commercial studio pottery kilns are produced in various sizes and designs. "Portable" kilns are assembled at the factory, shipped as a unit, and installed with local labor. "Permanent type" kilns are erected on the site by company engineers with plans and materials furnished by the manufacturer. Some manufacturers will sell drawings and materials and allow the purchaser to construct his own kiln.

Where suitable power supply is available the electric kiln has many advantages for the individual potter. It is safe, quiet, convenient, easy to operate, and free from the dangers of changing kiln atmospheres and combustion gases. The least expensive electric kilns make use of "Nichrome" metallic heating elements and have a maximum temperature limit of 2000° F (cone 04). This type of kiln is adequate for many kinds of local clays, and specially prepared low-temperature clay bodies, but higher temperatures are necessary for the more durable stoneware and porcelain. Electric kilns for these wares make use of heating elements of non-metallic silicon-carbide, called "glo-bars." *

It must not be expected that a kiln will give perfect service under all conditions or in the hands of an indifferent operator. No kiln will do that, but any well-constructed kiln can be relied upon to do excellent work in the hands of a careful and conscientious potter.

A kiln of the proper type, having been purchased, must be carefully installed. For a fuel-burning kiln a good chimney is an absolute necessity. A strong draft is essential for the proper burning of gravity-fed oil, or for vapor fuel which does not make use of mechanical mixers or blowers. The chimney should be at least 25 feet high and should be lined with fire brick to a height of 6 feet above the entry.

---

* Harper Electric Furnace Company, Niagara Falls, N. Y.

The kiln room should have a cement floor and should be well drained and well ventilated. A stout bench should be provided where the work of preparation may be done, and at a convenient spot there should be shelves for stilts, cones, kiln wash, and all the minor accessories of firing. If the room is fireproof, insurance rates will not be greatly affected.

If the chosen kiln is the prefabricated or portable variety it should be inspected to see if the muffle or fire box has been damaged in transit. It is a good plan to make up a wash of kaolin and brush thickly over the floor of the kiln. The side walls may also be coated but with a thinner application. This protects the interior of the kiln from the attacks of glaze.

In order to fill the kiln economically, proper "kiln furniture" must be provided to support the ware. This is usually an assortment of refractory shelves and supports and may be obtained from the manufacturer or from dealers in refractory materials. These shelves may be used even when broken, as two or more may be used to bridge the width of the kiln. The upper surfaces of shelves should be protected with kiln wash. Kiln furniture may be leveled by inserting small wads of fire clay which has been mixed with equal parts of crushed, burned fire brick, called "grog."

The new kiln should be given a preliminary drying out by burning a very low flame. The length of the drying period will vary with the size and type of kiln. A few hours will be sufficient for a small portable kiln, but a large freshly constructed masonry kiln may require several days. At any rate the first firing of the kiln should be with pieces of no great importance. The behavior of the kiln must be observed and the temperature in various parts of the kiln must be ascertained. In order to do this a number of pyrometric cones are prepared in groups of three.

Let us suppose that the work is intended to be carried out at a temperature of Cone No. 01. The cone numbers run both ways from this. The higher or less fusible cones are 1, 2, 3, 4, etc., up to 36 and the more fusible, lower cone numbers are 02, 03, 04, etc., down to 022. The lowest cone, 022, begins to bend soon after the kiln heat has reached the stage of visible redness. The highest cone, 36, will soften only at white incandescence and requires specially constructed furnaces. It is used only for testing materials and in problems of research. If the firing is to be cone 01, numbers 02, 01 and 1 are selected and set upright in a small strip of soft clay. Eight or ten of these groups of three cones are to be prepared for the first firing, so as to test the kiln, one group is placed in each corner, at the bottom, and another on each corner on a shelf, which is arranged opposite the spy hole in the door.

The kiln is now filled with pieces of pottery. To burn an empty kiln is not a reliable test. On the first occasion the firing should be started in the morning because no one can tell just how long the burn will take. When this time is ascertained it is best to start the fire so that the kiln will be finished by early evening. The cooling then takes place at night and there is no temptation to open the door too soon. Let us now start the fire very low and while the kiln is warming up we will take time out to learn what is happening in our kiln. First—let us consider the fire.

It is important that anyone attempting to burn a kiln should have some understanding of combustion. Many things occur in the firing which, without such an understanding, are not easily explained, but which become perfectly clear when considered in the light of elementary science.

Combustion means oxidation or a combination between the elements of the fuel, principally carbon and hydrogen, and the oxygen of the air. This combination is a chemical action and as it proceeds heat is liberated. With a given amount of a specific fuel and a given amount of air there is always the same amount of heat, but the rate at which this heat is given off varies with the time occupied in the operation. Heat may be generated slowly which means a low temperature, or the same volume of heat may be generated rapidly, occupying a much shorter time and developing a higher temperature. From these statements it will be seen that there is a difference between *heat* and *temperature*. Heat means quantity, temperature means intensity. Thus the temperature which can be obtained from a given amount of fuel depends upon the rapidity with which it is burned.

Combustion may be complete or incomplete. In the former case enough air is supplied to oxidize all the fuel, with, usually, some excess. The contents of the kiln are then bathed in the heated oxygen and the condition of the burning is called oxidizing. When the combustion is incomplete, on the other hand, there is a deficiency of oxygen, the kiln is charged with hot carbonaceous gases and smoke, and these, being hungry for oxygen, will attract it from any substance which may be present. This condition is called "reducing" because the compounds which exist in clay or glaze are deprived of oxygen and thus reduced to a lower state of oxidation.

In burning a kiln one should be able to produce either of these conditions at will because there are certain wares which require one or the other in order to secure the best results. To put the matter simply, oxidizing conditions are induced by a strong draft and open flues; reducing conditions are obtained by closing the air inlets and using a liberal amount of fuel.

What effect does the firing process have on our clay pieces and what are the changes which occur?

In order to answer these questions we must examine the nature of the clay. All clay contains water in two different relationships—physical and chemical water. The physical water is variable in quantity and can be seen. It is the water which wets our clay and provides its workability. Physical water, sometimes called "water of plasticity," can be removed by prolonged drying in an oven. But if we should stop our firing at that point the clay can always be wet and worked again and nothing permanent has been accomplished.

The chemical water, on the other hand, is invisible, constant, and locked into the chemical constituency of the clay. It cannot be removed by drying alone, but must be burned or fired until the clay reaches a glowing red heat throughout its entire mass. When that point is reached our clay has not only been dried, it has been "dehydrated," and can never again be made plastic by wetting.

Clay also contains carbonaceous animal and vegetable matter, which must be removed by oxidation. The process begins as soon as the clay is red hot, and in the case of very heavy ware, may continue for several hours. Some native red clays are rich in carbonaceous matter and therefore require a longer time for complete oxidation.

Many types of primitive wares were given no further heat treatment than dehydration and oxidation. But the making of durable, permanent ware calls for another quality—namely, that of density or vitrification. This is the final stage in firing and consists of the melting or softening of the heat responsive fluxes or minerals within the clay structure. The volume shrinkage of our ware begins during the early stages of vitrification. Since the mineral composition of clays is variable, each clay will have its own "firing range," or margin of safety, beyond which it may lose its form and become liquid. The potter must determine for himself the point at which his clay will become sufficiently dense for his purposes, and at that point the clay is said to be "mature" and the firing is finished.

The heat work to be accomplished—namely, water drying, dehydration, oxidation, and vitrification—requires that the potter have due regard for time as well as temperature. Damp ware will burst if heated too rapidly. Heavy ware requires a more gradual heat treatment than thin ware. Insufficient time for oxidation may cause certain clays to blacken and bloat. Underfired clay will be soft and porous and overfired clay may become distorted and otherwise lose its form.

The performance of the kiln can be evaluated and results can be easily checked if an accurate record or time-temperature "chart" is kept during each firing. Data on fuel consumption and burner adjustments will also be helpful in subsequent firings.

As the kiln approaches redness the cones in front of the spy hole will become visible, and in a few hours the color will be a bright cherry red and cone number 02 will begin to bend at the tip and will gradually arch over until the point touches the shelf upon which the cones stand.   By this time number 01 will have begun to bend and when the point of this has touched the shelf, the firing is assumed to be complete and the fuel is shut off.

It requires some resolution to leave a kiln until morning but it is conducive to early rising anyway.   The kiln need not be quite cold but it will help the kiln itself to wear better and the pottery will be better if nothing is done until everything can be handled without gloves.

The cones are now taken out and a diagram is made of each level with the bend of each cone accurately drawn. This diagram should be mounted and hung on the wall for reference.   It is not well to trust to memory.   With some kilns it may be found that the cones on the bottom have bent further than those on the shelf.   That is, the bottom is somewhat hotter.   The condition of the fired ware in various parts of the kiln should be carefully observed.

The variation in the kiln is not necessarily a disadvantage.   It may be utilized in burning wares of different kinds.   For example, if the bottom proves much the hotter, the biscuit ware may be placed below and the glazed pieces on the shelf.   In such cases the shelf should be washed with a good coating of clay and flint in order to protect it from casual drops of glaze.

If a number of small pieces are being made, more than

one shelf should be set up. The legs may be just a little taller than the tallest of the small pieces, but the art of placing or filling a kiln economically consists in making a selection of pieces which fit well together both as regards height and shape. Thus, pieces which are large at the base may be dovetailed in with others of which the base is smaller than the upper part. In the case of clay ware the pieces may be set close together or even piled one upon another. There is no danger of sticking unless the ware is burned to complete vitrification. The glazed pieces must not, of course, touch each other.

It will be seen, from these instructions, that there should be a good assortment of wares from which to select. Economical firing cannot be managed if a burn is attempted whenever a piece is ready, and patience must be exercised so as to fill the kiln to advantage.

Chapter XIV

HIGH–TEMPERATURE WARES

HARD–FIRED wares are divided into two classes, porcelain and stoneware. Both these wares are fired once, technically; that is, the body and glaze come to maturity at one and the same burning. The biscuit ware is often given a low burn at first in order to facilitate handling, but this leaves the body very porous and is in no sense a maturing fire. The glaze is laid upon this porous ware, or upon the unburned clay if preferred, and then comes the high fire.

A mix for a porcelain body has already been given, but if the ceramist means seriously to attack the porcelain problem he will have to do some experimental work for himself. The Georgia kaolin mentioned in the recipe on page 26 is a good, plastic clay but it is slightly off color. It may be necessary to improve the color by the use, in part, of another kaolin.

Furthermore, in the preparation of a fine porcelain it is necessary to grind the whole mix upon a mill. The mill used for glaze grinding will answer every purpose and care must be taken that the grinding, while carried far enough, be not too long continued. A certain amount of fine grit in the body mass is necessary but only by constant practice can the right point be reached. In making these experiments each step should be faithfully noted in a handy book. The amount of water to a given weight of clay and the duration of the grinding should be accurately observed and written down. It is most unwise to trust to memory.

The process of casting may be used for porcelain as already described, but the very best of workmanship is necessary. The hard fire to which the porcelain is subjected reveals every error which has occurred in the making. The same thing applies to wheel work. Not only is great skill required in order to shape the tender porcelain clay on the wheel but the very essence of the porcelain is its lightness, to produce which by craftsmanship a long and arduous course of training must be endured.

Stoneware is free from many of these difficulties and, consequently, one who attempts the conquest of high-temperature wares is advised to begin with this. Stoneware clay need not be a mixture. There are many clays which can be used for the manufacture of grès with no more preparation than that laid down for common clays. It sometimes happens that a clay will need the addition of a small quantity of flint or spar but this does not amount to a difficulty.

Stoneware does not present the same manufacturing difficulties as are found in porcelain. The clay is quite plastic and can be shaped easily on the wheel; casting is scarcely a suitable process for this ware. The essence of stoneware is strength and virility, just as that of porcelain is lightness and grace. Each ware has forms suited to itself and it is a mistake to depart from these essential characteristics.

After shaping and drying the technical manipulation of both wares proceeds along the usual lines. The first fire is at a very low temperature. The melting point of silver (cone 010) is enough in nearly every case. This leaves the ware in a soft and porous condition but hard enough to resist the action of water. The process of glazing has already been described but the composition of the proper glazes differs from that of low-temperature glazes.

Porcelain is always burned in a reducing fire; stoneware may be burned either reducing or oxidizing. The temperature at which the glaze is burned is very high, it must be, in fact, the maturing point of the body itself.

The simplest form of porcelain glaze is that represented by the formula—

$$\left. \begin{array}{l} K_2O \dots \dots .3 \\ CaO \dots \dots .7 \end{array} \right\} \quad Al_2O_3 \dots \dots .5 \quad SiO_2 \dots \dots 4.0$$

which is carried out in the following mixture:

Feldspar	167
Whiting	70
Kaolin	52
Flint	108

The glaze is ground for use.

The same glaze will also serve for stoneware but it will burn to a brilliant surface whereas stoneware is better when finished with a matt texture.

The following is a stoneware matt glaze:

$$\left. \begin{array}{l} K_2O \dots \dots .3 \\ CaO \dots \dots .7 \end{array} \right\} \quad Al_2O_3 \dots \dots .7 \quad SiO_2 \dots \dots 2.6$$

of which formula the mixture is—

Feldspar	167
Whiting	70
Calcined Kaolin	66
Raw Kaolin	26

The porcelain glaze is at its best when uncolored. The matt glaze will be more interesting when used as a colored coating.

The following are a few suggestions for colored matt stoneware glazes. To the glaze batch, 329 parts, add:

For blue:
    Cobalt Oxide........................... 2 parts
    Nickel Oxide........................... 1 part
    Ground Rutile.......................... 10 parts

For brown:
    Iron Oxide............................. 6 parts
    Nickel Oxide........................... 3 parts
    Ground Rutile.......................... 10 parts

For green:
    Chrome Oxide.......................... 2 parts
    Cobalt Oxide........................... 1 part
    Iron Oxide............................. 4 parts

For dark red:
    Iron Oxide............................. 10 parts
    Chrome Oxide.......................... 2 parts
    Zinc Oxide............................. 6 parts

Rutile has not been mentioned before. It is a crude oxide of titanium and is exceedingly useful in high-temperature work for producing odd, mossy and crystalline effects.

These mixtures make no pretense to be complete, they are given as suggestions only because if the artist-potter is to be successful he must be prepared to compound glazes which are the expression of his own individuality.

For burning high-temperature wares the kilns already described may be used but upon purchasing the stipulation should be made that the kiln is to stand burning up to cone 11 or 12. Successful porcelain can be made at cone 10 but better results are secured at cone 12, although, of course, the wear upon the kiln is proportionately greater. Stoneware requires a burn of about cone 9, higher or lower according to the clay used but fine results must not be expected below cone 7 nor is it necessary to go higher than cone 10.

There are a number of firms who deal in ceramic supplies and equipment for amateur craftsmen, schools, and semi-professional producers. As a rule small orders are not attractive to the larger suppliers of industry, but some have organized special departments for that purpose. For the most part, however, the equipment of the average individual potter or school can be met by firms dealing in general ceramic supplies. The following brief list of suppliers may be supplemented by reference to the various ceramic trade publications.

General Supplies . . Allied Engineering Co.
Cleveland, Ohio
O. Hommel Company
Pittsburgh, Pa.
B. F. Drakenfeld
New York, N. Y.
L. H. Butcher Co.
2638 East Olympic Boulevard
Los Angeles, Calif.
American Art Clay Co.
Indianapolis, Ind.

Clays . . . . United Clay Mines, Trenton, N. J.

Kilns . . . . Allied Engineering Co., Cleveland, Ohio
Denver Fireclay Co., Denver, Colo.
Harper Electric Furnace Co., Niagara Falls, N. Y.

American Art Clay Company, Indianapolis, Ind.

Equipment for
Processing and
Forming Clay ..Crossley Manufacturing Co., Trenton, N. J.
Patterson Foundry and Machine Co., East Liverpool, Ohio

Periodicals and Trade Literature:
Bulletins and *Journal of the American Ceramic Society*, Columbus, Ohio
Ceramic Industry, 59 East Van Buren Street, Chicago, Ill.
Ceramic Age, 421 Parker Street, Newark 4, N. J.

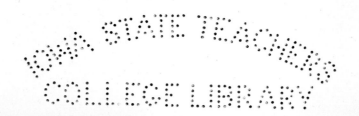

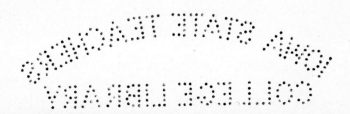

INDEX